JAMES M. REID, JR., and ANNE SILLECK

BETTER BUSINESS LETTERS

**A Programed Book
to Develop Skill in Writing**

ADDISON-WESLEY PUBLISHING COMPANY
Reading, Massachusetts · Menlo Park, California · London · Don Mills, Ontario

The illustrations, by Lou Fine, were supplied by the author.

ISBN 0-201-06306
GHIJKLMNOP-AL-79876543

CONTENTS

The back cover is perforated so that a portion can be torn off and used as an answer mask.

ACKNOWLEDGMENTS

We would like to thank Mr. E. J. Feeney, Assistant Vice President–Sales, of Emery Air Freight Corporation; Mrs. Cecelia L. Baros, Assistant Training Specialist, Personnel Training, of The Prudential Insurance Company of America; Mr. Robert Jud, Assistant Vice President, Skills Training Division, of Bankers Trust Company; and Mr. Malcolm W. Warren, Manager of Training and Development, Questor Corporation, for their cooperation in administering the field test of our manuscript. Our thanks also go to the employees of the above firms who actually worked through the manuscript and gave us the data and comments with which to make final revisions.

We would especially like to express our appreciation to Mrs. Linn Harding, whose attention to detail has helped us immensely in the production of this book.

Mr. Lou Fine is the artist responsible for the excellent drawings.

West Redding, Conn.   J.M.R., Jr.
August 1969   A.S.

TO THE INSTRUCTOR

ABOUT THE BOOK

This programed book is designed to help your students develop skill in writing business letters. It is called a program because it uses programed instruction—a method of teaching which requires the student to respond in writing as he learns.

A quick glance at the material will show that it is different from that in a conventional text. For one thing, the subject matter is presented in a series of small steps. Each step, called a "frame," gives the student some information and then requires him to answer a question or practice a writing skill. After the student has answered, he can uncover the correct answer and learn whether he is right or not. The whole process is much like conversing with an instructor who asks questions and tells the student when he answers correctly.

This book has been developed in consultation with people in business and industry and has been field-tested under conditions of actual use in four different firms.

OBJECTIVES

Although we make no claim that this book "will teach your students how to write," we do believe that it will achieve the limited behavioral objectives it was designed to achieve. These objectives are listed below, lesson by lesson.

Lesson 1: Writing Concise Sentences. In this lesson the student learns to . . .
    . . . detect and eliminate unnecessary words or phrases,
    . . . detect and revise wordy phrases and redundancies.

Lesson 2: Keeping Your Reader's Interest
Part I. In this lesson the student learns to . . .
    . . . detect general words and to substitute more exact, specific ones,
    . . . distinguish between sentences written in the passive voice and those in the active voice,
    . . . convert passive sentences to active ones.

Part II. In this lesson the student learns to . . .
    . . . use the appropriate link (*and, or, however,* etc.) to indicate the relationship between ideas,
    . . . detect errors in the use of parallelism and correct them.

Lesson 3: Being Natural, Courteous, and Personal. In this lesson the student learns
to . . .
. . . detect inflated language and use simpler words,
. . . detect archaic business expressions and substitute more modern ones,
. . . use positive rather than negative language wherever possible,
. . . achieve a more personal tone by using a liberal sprinkling of "I," "you,"
and "we."

Lesson 4: The Start and the Finish. In this lesson the student learns to . . .
. . . write opening sentences which include an explanation of what the letter
is about, the idea of most interest to the reader (if possible), and the date
of the reader's letter (if applicable),
. . . write closing sentences which do not contain the usual insincere clichés
but which contain specific requests for action or summaries.

Lesson 5: Planning and Writing Your Letter. In this lesson the student learns to . . .
. . . detect and eliminate irrelevant ideas,
. . . make a "laundry list" of ideas for organization,
. . . salvage good will in a turn-down letter by using such devices as giving
reasons before the actual turn-down, assuring careful consideration, or
recommending positive alternatives.

HOW TO USE THIS BOOK

Anyone who must write business letters on the job will find this program useful.
However, to achieve best results, the students should have at least a high school
education.

The programed lessons can stand on their own as the sole means of instruction,
or they may be used in conjunction with other methods of instruction in a variety
of learning situations.

The book is composed of an Introduction and five programed lessons (Lesson 2
has two parts), each accompanied by a Quiz.

**Important: If you plan to administer the Quizzes formally, be sure to tear out
pages 169 through 177 in the back of each copy of the book *before* you distribute it to a student. These pages have the correct answers for scoring the
Quizzes.**

Each lesson should take *about* one hour for the student to complete and each Quiz
about one-half hour. However, individual students may vary from these times by as
much as 50%.

To achieve best results, we recommend that the program be administered in six
Sessions, as outlined below:

Approximate Study Time

Orientation	15 minutes	
Introduction and Lesson 1	60 minutes	
Quiz—Lesson 1	30 minutes	
SESSION 1		105 minutes
Lesson 2, Part I	60 minutes	
Quiz—Part I	30 minutes	
SESSION 2		90 minutes
Lesson 2, Part II	60 minutes	
Quiz—Part II	30 minutes	
SESSION 3		90 minutes
Lesson 3	60 minutes	
Quiz—Lesson 3	30 minutes	
SESSION 4		90 minutes
Lesson 4	60 minutes	
Quiz—Lesson 4	30 minutes	
SESSION 5		90 minutes
Lesson 5	60 minutes	
Quiz—Lesson 5	30 minutes	
SESSION 6		90 minutes
TOTAL TIME		555 minutes or 9 hours 15 minutes

As you can see, each session lasts about an hour and a half. To be on the safe side, allow about two hours for each session. We recommend that one session be given each day for a total of six days. If you want to condense the time that the students work on the program, we recommend that you give one session in the morning and one in the afternoon, for a total of three days. *We strongly recommend that you do not ask the student to do more than two sessions in one day.*

We suggest that you provide a quiet place where the students can work without interruptions. Programed instruction requires much concentration and its effectiveness is dissipated if a student must put down a lesson in the middle and pick it up later.

Before the students start reading the Introduction, we suggest that you give them a brief orientation:

1. Explain that they are being given a new kind of training material which will help them develop skills for writing better business letters. Tell them they will be required to write answers to questions as they work through the lessons. Be sure

to emphasize that the program is not a test of their knowledge but is a method of instruction which includes self-testing.

2. Explain that when they finish a lesson, they will be given a Quiz to see how much they have learned. This will help motivate them to work conscientiously.

3. Ask them to write their answers carefully in the spaces provided in the lessons. If they make a mistake, they should understand why they were wrong before going on.

4. Tell them to work through the material at their own pace, to follow instructions, and not to hurry.

After the orientation, have them read the Introduction and begin work on Lesson 1. When they are finished with Lesson 1, have them take the Quiz for Lesson 1 in the back of the book. When they have finished, score the Quiz according to the correct answers in the back of the book. The test results should be discussed with the students.

Repeat this procedure for all lessons.

INTRODUCTION

Do you write good business letters?

That's not an easy question for most of us. Perhaps one way to find an answer is to ask yourself, "How does my business letter affect the person who reads it?"

Does it *confuse* him?

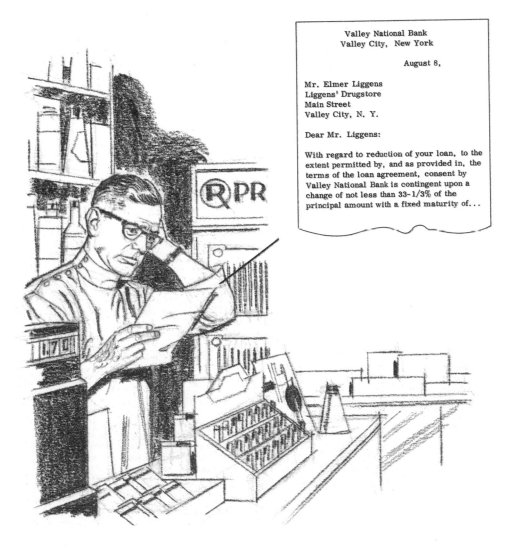

Valley National Bank
Valley City, New York

August 8,

Mr. Elmer Liggens
Liggens' Drugstore
Main Street
Valley City, N. Y.

Dear Mr. Liggens:

With regard to reduction of your loan, to the extent permitted by, and as provided in, the terms of the loan agreement, consent by Valley National Bank is contingent upon a change of not less than 33-1/3% of the principal amount with a fixed maturity of...

OR . . .

Does it make him *mad*?

The Judicial Insurance Co.
11 Madison Avenue
New York City, New York

April 11,

Mrs. Alice Jones
10 Black Rock Turnpike
Redding, Conn.

Dear Mrs. James:

Company policy dictates that we cannot possibly grant your request for a change of beneficiary for your husband's life insurance policy (#48-576-8372). In your letter of March 8, you claim that your husband gave you power of attorney, but...

OR . . .

Does it *bore* him?

Management Consultants, Inc.
1186 Wilshire Blvd.
Los Angeles, Calif.

March 2,

Mr. Thomas Thackery
President
Regent Manufacturing Co.
1011 King St.
Los Angeles, Calif.

Dear Mr. Thackery:

Enclosed herewith please find a presentation of systematized concepts which may be of interest in the area of determining savings in production line efficiency--both as to the time factor and the monetary factor. Our firm is at the present time engaged in operating a functionalized system of reciprocal analysis which may achieve optimal results on an integrated basis...

OR . . .

Does it do the job that you want it to?

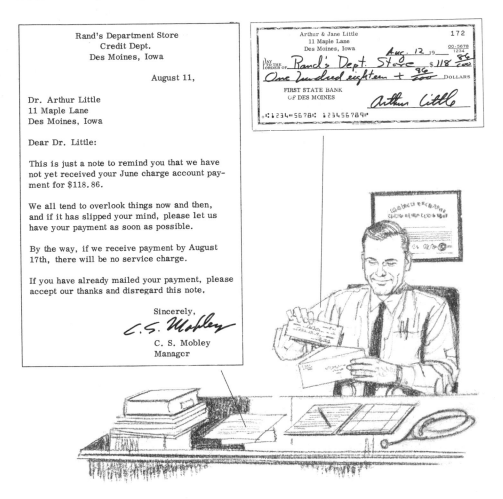

The point, of course, is that the best way to measure how well you write business letters is to see how well they accomplish their purposes. If a large percentage of your letters fail to do what you want them to—to affect the reader exactly as you intend—then you can probably use some improvement in your letter-writing skills.

THREE PURPOSES OF YOUR BUSINESS LETTERS

Many of your business letters have three basic purposes. The first and most obvious is to inform the reader—to communicate ideas and facts as accurately as possible from your mind to that of the reader. Thus, you will often find business letters with such sentences as the following:

I will be staying at the Clinton Hotel during the week of January 7th.

We shipped 300,000 barrels of crude oil via the Erie Railroad on August 8. The shipment should arrive in Jersey City by the 24th.

I am happy to tell you that Regent Magazine *has decided to buy your article at the price we asked.*

A second purpose of many of your letters is to prod the reader into doing something. Thus, business letters often contain sentences such as these:

Since I am very much interested in exploring some of the ideas we discussed recently, please call me at OXford 7-6852 and we can arrange a meeting.

If the shipment does not arrive by the 24th, send me a wire, and I will look into the problem.

Please sign the three copies of the contract and return them to me at the above address.

Not so obvious is the third purpose of most business letters—to make a good impression on the reader. Do many of your letters contain sentences such as the following?

Thank you for filling in and returning Form #308 so promptly.

I appreciate your efforts in behalf of Mr. Sears.

Please send the information to the following people: . . .

One of the purposes of such sentences is to create in the reader's mind a favorable image of the writer and his firm.

THE IMPORTANCE OF WRITING LETTERS THAT DO THE JOB

Most writers of business letters recognize the importance of informing the reader and of obtaining desired action from him because the achievement of these purposes is essential to the proper conduct of a firm's business. Letters are a major expense for many organizations. In fact, it has been estimated that they cost about $3.50 each and that some companies spend more than a million dollars a year on them. No firm wants to waste its communications dollars by sending letters that do not fully inform and do not get the action they should. Unclear or unpersuasive letters represent wasted time and money and often require expensive follow-up letters.

Equally important as informing the reader and getting the proper action from him is making a good impression on him. Letters which do this are usually much more effective in accomplishing the other two objectives. Moreover, such letters often have two important side effects. First, they create a climate which helps your firm sell the reader its goods or services. Perhaps your letters do not have anything to do with selling, but they can help sales by increasing the number of people who have a favorable image of your firm. Second, letters that build good will can help your career, and letters that do not can hinder it. For example, would you like your boss to receive something like the following?

June 10

Mr. Thomas Sloan
Manager
Adjustments Dept.
Connelly's Dept. Store
Boston, Massachusetts

Dear Mr. Sloan:

I am writing to you about an extremely insulting letter which I just received from one of your employees, Mr. James Weed. I'm an adult and I expect to be so treated. Mr. Weed, however, seems to think I deserve a slap on the wrist because I thought your store should pay for repairs on a watch that I dropped. Mr. Weed may be right about the guarantee not covering breakage, but he doesn't have to be so snide about it.

You may be interested to know that I am taking the watch to a reputable jeweler to have it repaired at my own expense. I am also taking my business, which is considerable, to Allen's Department Store in the future.

Sincerely,

Mrs. Anne Turner

Or would you rather have him receive the following?

June 10

Mr. Thomas Sloan
Manager
Adjustments Dept.
Connelly's Dept. Store
Boston, Mass.

Dear Mr. Sloan:

This letter is to authorize you to make the necessary repairs on my watch and to charge the expense to my account.

Also, I would like to say that I have never been turned down in such a nice way as Mr. James Weed did. I had originally asked your store to pay for the repairs under the guarantee. But Mr. Weed explained that the guarantee did not cover breakage. His letter was so courteous and clear that I could not help but accept defeat graciously.

In this day and age, when one is constantly bombarded by words written by inept robots, Mr. Weed's letter came as a welcome relief.

Sincerely,

Mrs. Anne Turner

THE QUALITIES OF BETTER BUSINESS LETTERS

What should a good business letter be like? At a minimum, it should be—

CLEAR

CONCISE

WELL-ORGANIZED

NATURAL

COURTEOUS

PERSONAL

Let's discuss these qualities one by one. *Clarity,* of course, is essential if your letter is to achieve its purpose. The reader must understand exactly what your letter is trying to communicate. With this in mind, examine the following:

Dear Mr. Apdecker:

Contingent upon approval of those concerned, the remuneration of an individual partner for profit-sharing purposes will be deemed to be such proportion of the total available remuneration of all partners as the proportion of each partner's capital investment.

Now compare it with this:

Dear Mr. Apdecker:

If all three partners so agree, each partner will share in the profits in proportion to his initial capital investment. For instance, if Partner A invests $10,000 and Partners B and C invest $5,000 each, Partner A will receive one-half the profit while Partners B and C will receive one-quarter of the profit each.

This second version is much more likely to achieve its objective of informing the reader. Granted, very little writing is as muddy as the first example above, but if a letter leaves the reader any room for doubt, it may not accomplish its purposes.

Today, when most readers are inundated by a tremendous flow of written communication, *conciseness* is given high priority. People want to know what you have to say to them, as quickly as possible. This means saying it in the fewest words. It does not mean that your letters should be short or abrupt: a novel can be concise, while a single sentence can be unnecessarily wordy. Rather, conciseness is saying everything you have to say, without losing clarity or courtesy, in the fewest possible words.

Inconcise: It is hoped that word from Mr. Lewis in connection with the completion
of the project will be received by us at an early date.   (25 words)
Concise: We hope to hear soon from Mr. Lewis about completing the project.
(12 words, a saving of 13)

The concise sentence above says the same thing as the inconcise one in less than
half the number of words. Imagine reading a letter filled with sentences such as
the first one. You would probably be bored or irritated no matter how interesting
the contents of the letter were.

Saying that a letter should be *well-organized* is saying that it should be thoroughly
thought out. You should not sit down to think of what you will write but to write what
you have thought. In other words, you can't expect your letter to be either clear or
concise unless you have weeded out irrelevant ideas, chosen relevant ideas, and
arranged them in an effective order. For example, suppose you are answering a
letter of inquiry. In order to obtain the necessary information, you have to go to
the company library and credit files, and you talk with several executives about the
letter. Should you inform your reader of all this research? Probably not. The
reader is primarily interested in the information you have obtained for him, not how
you obtained it. Thus, if your letter opens, "Upon receiving your letter I went to
the company library and also looked in our credit files . . . ," you would probably
be writing a disorganized letter.

One of the most common faults of business letter writers is their tendency to use
archaic, pompous, or inflated language. This flowery writing style was acceptable
over 70 years ago. For instance, below is a letter from a book of models of business
letters published in 1804. The book is called *Payne's Business Letter Writer and
Book of Commercial Forms.* This example letter is from a fruit broker to a potential
customer.

New York, May 1st, 1885
No. 50 Front St.

MESSRS. POPHAM, MAYO & CO.
No. 55 Beaver St., New York

GENTLEMEN: I beg to inform you that I have this day opened an office at the
above number for transaction of business as broker in fruits and spices.

The knowledge and experience gained in 15 years, while in the employ of
Messrs. Stark Bros. & Co., enables me to give you every assurance, while
soliciting your countenance and support, that all orders entrusted to me for
execution will receive my most careful attention.

Referring to Messrs. S. B. & Co., my late employers, as above, and Messrs.
Dows, Cattlin & Co., of Front St.,

I remain, respectfully,

Your obedient servant,

Wording such as "I beg to inform you" and "in the employ of" was customary in the business world of long ago, but it is no longer appropriate for the modern business-man. Nonetheless, such pompous, archaic usage still may be found in a surprisingly large number of business letters. For this reason, we emphasize that a business letter should be written in a *natural,* conversational style that does not call attention to itself at the expense of the ideas and facts you are trying to communicate.

A business letter must be not only natural but *courteous.* Courtesy to the reader is not just a matter of including such words as "please" and "thank you"—although they play an important part in being courteous—but it is also being positive rather than negative. Courtesy is saying, "We will try to have your toaster repaired by August 6," rather than, "We cannot have your toaster repaired until August 6." More important, courtesy is your attitude toward the reader. If you have a friendly, helpful feeling for the reader, your letter cannot help but reflect this attitude.

The last quality on our list is being *personal.* Your business letter should be a personal communication between two people rather than an impersonal notice from one statistic to another. This is particularly important today because as companies and other organizations become larger and more powerful, individuals become more sensitive to any suggestion that the organization or its representative does not *care.* So when you write a business letter, you should strive to visualize your reader —to see him as a person with feelings of his own and with problems and needs that are a little different from those of his fellows.

We believe then, that these are the five qualities which make for better business letters.

ABOUT THIS BOOK

This book consists of five lessons which can help you gain skill in writing better business letters. Each lesson has been programed. That is, the material is pre-sented in small steps called *frames.* Each frame presents some information and then requires you to answer a question or practice a writing skill. After you have written your answer, you can uncover the correct answer and learn whether you were right or not. This whole process is much like talking with an instructor who asks you questions and tells you when you are right.

Each frame is designed so that you will answer correctly most of the time—to help you learn. Programed instruction is *not* a test; it is a method of teaching which includes self-testing.

Now, a few words of advice:

1. Take your time. Read each frame carefully and work at your own pace. Each lesson should take about an hour, but don't worry if you take more or less time because we know that people learn at different rates and still may acquire the same amount of information and skill.

2. Each frame has enough space for you to write your answer directly on the page. When you get a wrong answer, reread the frame to understand why you were wrong.
3. A programed book, unlike a conventional text, cannot be scanned, crammed, or skipped. Nor should you begin in the middle of a lesson. Begin each lesson at the beginning and don't stop until you come to the end. Before you begin a lesson, be sure you have enough time to finish—about one hour.
4. You will need a pencil while working through the lessons.

LESSON 1 | WRITING CONCISE SENTENCES

As we mentioned in the Introduction, a concise sentence says what has to be said in the fewest number of words—without losing clarity or courtesy. This lesson will help you write concise sentences by showing you how to recognize and eliminate some typical cases of business verbosity.

Tear off the mask from the back cover of this book and place it over this page so that the top edge lies just beneath the solid line below. Lower the mask slowly until you uncover a dotted line. Please do not go below this line until you have written your answer in the space provided.

UNNECESSARY WORDS AND PHRASES

Begin to study here.

↓

1a

Some words and phrases that often crop up in business letters do nothing to carry the meaning of a sentence to the reader. Such unnecessary verbiage should be ruthlessly cut out with the stroke of a pen. Read the example below.

Please be advised that your payment arrived on June 13th.   (10 words)

Is the phrase "please be advised that" necessary to the meaning of this sentence?

_____*No*_____ *C*

↑

Write *yes* or *no* in this space and then lower your mask to the next dotted line.

Stop here . . . . **Stop here**

Check your answer with this correct answer.

no ↵

1b

Rewrite the example sentence above so that it is concise. _*Your payment*_

C arrived on June 13th.

. . . .

Your payment arrived on June 13th.   (6 words, a saving of 4)

or

We received your payment on June 13th.   (7 words, a saving of 3)

Following the same procedure, continue to study here.

↓

2

 ~~I wish to tell you that~~ our meeting for the 4th has been postponed to the 16th.

(17 words)

Cross out the phrase that can be eliminated from the above sentence without changing its meaning.

. . . .

~~I wish to tell you that~~ our meeting for the 4th has been postponed to the 16th.

(11 words, a saving of 6)

3

In each of the following sentences, cross out the unnecessary phrase.

A. Our research department is making a study ~~along the lines~~ of microbiotics.

B. ~~It happened that~~ your electric iron did not arrive within the 90-day warranty period.

C. We have a high turnover rate because ~~of the fact that~~ our employees can readily find new jobs.

D. We expect sales to rise about three ~~or four~~ percent next month.

. . . .

A. Our research department is making a study ~~along the lines~~ of microbiotics.

B. ~~It happened that~~ your electric iron did not arrive within the 90-day warranty period.

C. We have a high turnover rate because ~~of the fact that~~ our employees can readily find new jobs.

D. We expect sales to rise ~~about~~ three or four percent next month. ("Three or four percent" is indefinite enough. "About" adds nothing.)

or

We expect sales to rise about three ~~or four~~ percent next month. ("About three" or "about four" is indefinite enough. "About three or four" is wordy.)

4

When you are expressing an opinion (as opposed to an objective statement of fact), it is often helpful to use such expressions as "I think . . . ," "It is my opinion that . . . ," or "We feel that . . . ." However, you are being wordy when you use such expressions as "I *personally* think . . ." because an opinion cannot be anything *but* personal.

In each of the following sentences, cross out the unnecessary word.

    A.   We are looking for a receptionist with a pleasant ~~sounding~~ voice.

    B.   I <u>personally</u> think that the ~~present~~ slump in prices is temporary.

    C.   Mr. Manner, our former president, is ~~located~~ with American Motors.

    D.   This new breed of mice can be effectively used for medical research ~~purposes.~~

. . . .

    A.   We are looking for a receptionist with a pleasant ~~sounding~~ voice.

    B.   I ~~personally~~ think that the present slump in prices is temporary.

    C.   Mr. Manner, our former president, is ~~located~~ with American Motors.

    D.   This new breed of mice can be effectively used for medical research ~~purposes.~~

5

The following sentences may or may not contain one or more unnecessary words or phrases. Cross them out wherever they occur.

X A. ~~We think~~ our laboratories are well equipped.

B. It's my ~~personal~~ opinion that the current trend in sales is unfavorable.

C. The Board of Directors plans to meet in ~~about~~ two or three weeks for further discussion ~~along the lines~~ of a merger with Regent Corporation.

D. ~~Please be advised that~~ machine-tool orders are up ~~about~~ six percent this month.

X E. ~~Please~~ let us hear from you soon.

X F. We are ~~now~~ located at 117 Springdale Road.

G. My secretary, ~~whose name is~~ Mrs. McDonald, will be going to Europe for three weeks for ~~purposes of~~ a vacation.

. . . .

A. We think our laboratories are well equipped.

B. It's my ~~personal~~ opinion that the current trend in sales is unfavorable.

C. The Board of Directors plans to meet in ~~about~~ two or three weeks for further discussion ~~along the lines~~ of a merger with Regent Corporation.

or

The Board of Directors plans to meet in about two ~~or three~~ weeks for further discussion ~~along the lines~~ of a merger with Regent Corporation.

D. ~~Please be advised that~~ machine-tool orders are up about six percent this month.

E. Please let us hear from you soon.

F. We are now ~~located~~ at 117 Springdale Road.

G. My secretary, ~~whose name is~~ Mrs. McDonald, will be going to Europe for three weeks for ~~purposes of~~ a vacation.

6a

Cross out all unnecessary words or phrases in the following paragraph.

~~I wish to tell you that~~ an increase in prices is essential, which is due to ~~the fact that there has been~~ a rise in the cost of raw materials of ~~about~~ five or six percent. Moreover, our contract with the union expires July 31st, and discussions ~~along the lines of~~ a new contract are already under way. I ~~personally~~ think the union will not accept less than a two percent increase.

. . . .

~~I wish to tell you that~~ an increase in prices is essential, ~~which is~~ due to ~~the fact that there has been~~ a rise in the cost of raw materials of ~~about~~ five or six percent (or: . . . of about five ~~or six~~ percent). Moreover, our contract with the union expires July 31st, and discussions ~~along the lines~~ of a new contract are already under way. I ~~personally~~ think the union will not accept less than a two percent increase.

(An increase in prices is essential, due to a rise in the cost of raw materials of five or six percent. Moreover, our contract with the union expires July 31st, and discussions of a new contract are already under way. I think the union will not accept less than a two percent increase.)

6b

Which of the above two versions of this paragraph, the original or the revised version, best presents the writer's message? ___the revised___

. . . .

the revised version   (It's 19 words shorter.)

WORDY PHRASES

7a

Some phrases are wordy, but we cannot remove them from a sentence without changing its meaning. Such phrases should be revised to be more concise. Look at the following example.

I am in receipt of your letter of August 16th.

What is a shorter way of saying "I am in receipt of?" *I have Rec'd*

· ·

I received, I have received

7b

received

I ~~have here before me~~ your letter of August 16th.

Cross out the wordy phrase in the above sentence and write a shorter version over it.

· ·

received

I ~~have here before me~~ your letter of August 16th.

or

I have ~~here before me~~ your letter of August 16th.

8

soon.

Please let us hear from you ~~at an early date.~~

Cross out the wordy phrase in the above sentence and write a substitute word over your deletion.

· ·

soon, shortly

Please let us hear from you ~~at an early date.~~

9a

    A. I will consider the plans, as stated above, carefully.

    B. I will consider the above plans carefully.

Which of these two sentences is more concise, A or B? *B*

. . . .

    B

9b

    The figures, as indicated below, may have a 10% margin of error.

Rewrite this sentence so that it is more concise. *These figures indicated may have a 10% margin of error.*

    The following figures may have a 10% margin of error.

    or

    The figures below may have a 10% margin of error.

Throughout the rest of this book you will be asked to rewrite many of our examples. We would like to emphasize that your revisions do not have to correspond word for word with our answers in order for you to be correct. Our answers represent what *we think* are the best revisions in the given circumstances. Perhaps, when you are comparing your answers with ours, you may think that yours are a little better or you may find that ours are a little more effective than yours. In any case, when you are trying to judge whether your answer is *correct,* ask yourself these two questions: "Have I done what the authors have asked me to do?" "Have I kept the exact meaning of the original?"

10

We are hiring an efficiency expert in order that he may discover the cause of our production lag.

To shorten this sentence, you would cross out the phrase "in order that he may" and substitute the single word "__*to*__."

· ·

to

                             to

We are hiring an efficiency expert ~~in order that he may~~ discover the cause of our production lag.

11

My secretary recently wrote you in connection with our purchase of 20 gross of cotton yarn.

The phrase "in connection with" should be replaced by the word "*concerning*."

· ·

about, regarding, concerning

                            about

My secretary recently wrote you ~~in connection with~~ our purchase of 20 gross of cotton yarn.

12

Below is a list of wordy phrases. In the space provided after each phrase, write one word that can be substituted for it.

A. in the normal course of procedure _____ *usually* _____

✗ B. as a consequence of _____ *resulting* _____

C. at the present time _____ *now* _____

D. in the immediate future _____ *soon* _____

✗ E. during the time that _____ *then* _____   *(cont.)*

X F.   for the purpose of _____

. . . .

A.   normally, usually, ordinarily
B.   consequently, therefore, because of, due to
C.   presently, now, currently
D.   soon
E.   while, when
F.   to, for

13

Some of the following sentences contain wordy or unnecessary phrases. Cross them out and, when required, write your revision.

A.   We will consider your proposal ~~at an early date~~.   *soon.*

B.   We will answer you as soon as possible.

C.   We are considering the suggestion ~~contained~~ in your letter of October 23rd.

D.   The suggestions, ~~as stated~~ above, were received from union employees.

E.   ~~In the usual course of business~~ we serve ~~in the neighborhood~~ of 500 people   *about*
a day.

F.   Please distribute this memo through the usual channels.

. . . .

A.   We will consider your proposal ~~at an early date.~~   soon, shortly

B.   We will answer you as soon as possible.

C.   We are considering the suggestion ~~contained~~ in your letter of October 23rd.

D.   The suggestions ^ ~~, as stated above,~~ were received from union employees.   above

E.   ~~In the usual course of business~~ we serve ~~in the neighborhood of~~ 500 people   Usually, normally   about
a day.

F.   Please distribute this memo through the usual channels.

14

Draw a line from the phrase on the left to an appropriate substitute on the right.

A.	in the immediate future	1. therefore
B.	I am in receipt of	2. I received
C.	as a consequence of	3. soon
D.	at an early date	4. while
E.	I have here before me	5. following
F.	as stated below	6. now
G.	during the time that	7. to
H.	for the purpose of	8. usually
I.	at the present time	9. about
J.	in connection with	
K.	in order that he may	
L.	in the neighborhood of	
M.	in the normal course of procedure	

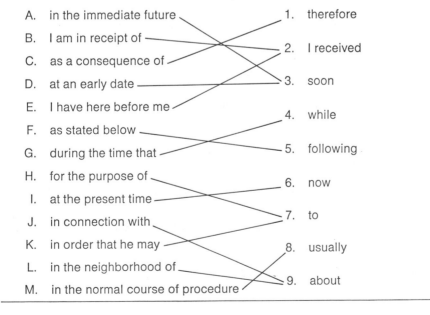

A.	in the immediate future	1. therefore
B.	I am in receipt of	2. I received
C.	as a consequence of	3. soon
D.	at an early date	4. while
E.	I have here before me	5. following
F.	as stated below	6. now
G.	during the time that	7. to
H.	for the purpose of	8. usually
I.	at the present time	9. about
J.	in connection with	
K.	in order that he may	
L.	in the neighborhood of	
M.	in the normal course of procedure	

15

Revise the following paragraph by crossing out the wordy phrases and writing in shorter versions.

I have ~~here before me~~ *received* your letter of the 16th requesting delivery of your order ~~in the immediate future~~ *soon*. ~~As a consequence of this~~ *therefore*, I have sent your shipment via air-freight instead of by rail as we would ~~in the normal course of procedure~~ *usual*.

· ·

I ~~have here before me~~ *received* your letter of the 16th requesting *immediate, early* delivery of your order ~~in the immediate future~~. ~~As a consequence of this~~ *Consequently, Therefore*, I have sent your shipment via air-freight instead of by rail as we *normally* would ~~in the normal course of procedure~~.

(I received your letter of the 16th requesting immediate delivery of your order. Consequently, I have sent your shipment via air-freight instead of by rail as we normally would.)

16a

WM. HARDCASTLE CO.
1670 Main Street

July 19

Frank Dixon

Partner

Appleby, Dixon & Pearsall—Civil Engineers

2930 Market Street

Dear Mr. Dixon:

~~Please be advised that~~ I have carefully considered your letter of the 16th, in
which you outline ~~in some detail~~ a *detailed* plan for ~~the matter of~~ automating our plant
~~located~~ at 26th Street. ~~As a consequence of this,~~ *therefore,* I have given your plan ~~into~~
to ~~the hands of~~ my assistant, ~~whose name is~~ John Masters, ~~in order that he may~~
to determine ~~whether or not it has~~ *finineal* practical *practicatily* ~~application for our~~ purposes ~~from a~~
~~financial viewpoint.~~

Mr. Masters ~~will be in touch with~~ *you* ~~you by~~ phone ~~by about~~ the first or second of
October ~~with regard to his determination.~~ *in the regard* If ~~it so happens that~~ you wish to
consult us at an earlier date ~~along the lines of~~ *regarding* his preliminary findings, I am
~~personally~~ sure he will be glad to answer any of your questions ~~in connection~~
~~with this matter.~~

Sincerely,

William Hardcastle

Is the above letter an example of concise writing? _____

. . . .

no

16b

Cross out any unnecessary or wordy phrases and write in appropriate revisions where required.

. . . .

~~Please be advised that~~ I have carefully considered your letter of the 16th, in

which you outline ~~in some detail~~ [detailed] a plan for ~~the matter of~~ automating our plant

~~located~~ at 26th Street. ~~As a consequence of this,~~ [Consequently] I have given your plan ~~into~~ [to]

~~the hands of~~ my assistant, ~~whose name is~~ John Masters, ~~in order that he may~~ [to]

determine [its financial practicality (or) whether it is financially practical.] ~~whether or not it has practical application for our purposes from a~~

~~financial viewpoint.~~

Mr. Masters will ~~be in touch with~~ [phone] you ~~by phone~~ by ~~about the first or second of~~ [October first or second]

~~October with regard to~~ [regarding, about] his determination. If ~~it so happens that~~ you wish to

consult us ~~at an earlier date along the lines of~~ [sooner] [about] his preliminary findings, I am

~~personally~~ sure he will be glad to answer any of your questions ~~in connection~~

~~with this matter.~~

(cont.)

16c

WM. HARDCASTLE CO.

1670 Main Street

July 19

Frank Dixon
Partner
Appleby, Dixon & Pearsall—Civil Engineers
2930 Market Street

Dear Mr. Dixon:

I have carefully considered your letter of the 16th, in which you outlined a detailed plan for automating our plant at 26th Street. Consequently, I have given your plan to my assistant, John Masters, to determine its financial practicality.

Mr. Masters will phone you on October first or second regarding his determination. If you wish to consult us sooner about his preliminary findings, he will be glad to answer any of your questions.

Sincerely,
William Hardcastle

Is the above revised letter an example of concise writing? _____ *yes*

. . . .

yes   (It's 64 words shorter.)

REDUNDANT WORDS AND PHRASES

17a

Phrases that say the same thing twice are redundant. Consider the following sentence:

> The basic fundamentals of our new marketing scheme are outlined in the enclosed brochure.

Fundamentals are by definition basic. Therefore, the revision should be:

> The basics of our new marketing scheme are outlined in the enclosed brochure.

> or

> The fundamentals of our new marketing scheme are outlined in the enclosed brochure.

Circle the redundant words in the following sentence.

It is the same identical approach we used last year.

· ·

It is the same identical approach we used last year.

17b

Using the answer above, cross out the unnecessary word in the circled phrase.

· ·

same ~~identical~~   or   ~~same~~ identical

18

Circle the redundant phrase in the following sentence and cross out the unnecessary word.

Because of this new discovery, we must start our research over again.

· ·

Because of this new discovery, we must start our research ~~over~~ again.

or

Because of this new discovery, we must start our research over ~~again.~~

19a

Circle the redundant phrases in the following sentence.

(Each and every) American should be taught the (basic fundamentals) of the law.

. . . .

(Each and every) American should be taught the (basic fundamentals) of the law.

19b

Now rewrite this sentence by filling in the blanks.

___*Every*___ American should be taught the ___*fundamentals*___ of the law.

. . . .

Each (or Every)
basics (or fundamentals)

20a

Circle all the redundant phrases in the following paragraph.

Much preliminary (thought and consideration) has gone into arranging our sales conference this year. The executive committee has decided that the (right and proper) approach to this conference should be to develop a (polite and courteous) attitude in our salesmen. A (full and complete) outline of the proposed agenda is enclosed.

. . . .

Much preliminary (thought and consideration) has gone into arranging our sales conference this year. The executive committee has decided that the (right and proper) approach to this conference should be to develop a (polite and courteous) attitude in our salesmen. A (full and complete) outline of the proposed agenda is enclosed.

20b

In each of the redundant phrases above, one word is sufficient to express the meaning. Rewrite the paragraph by filling in the blank spaces.

Much preliminary _Consideration_ has gone into arranging our sales conference this year. The executive committee has decided that the _proper_ _____ approach to this conference should be to develop a _courteous_ attitude in our salesmen. A _complete_ outline of the proposed agenda is enclosed.

· ·

thought (or consideration)   polite (or courteous)
right (or proper)   full (or complete)

21

Each of the following sentences contains a redundant phrase. Circle each of the redundant phrases and cross out the unnecessary word.

A.   The ~~true~~ facts speak for themselves.

B.   We are looking for a warehouse to rent because our stockrooms are too small ~~in size~~ to hold our expanded inventory.

C.   All applicants for this position must show due proof of age.

D.   We first began looking for a new site in 1965.

E.   The receipt will then be returned ~~back~~ to you.

· ·

A.   The ~~true~~ facts speak for themselves.

B.   We are looking for a warehouse to rent because our stockrooms are too small ~~in size~~ to hold our expanded inventory.

C.   All applicants for this position must show ~~due~~ proof of age.

D.   We ~~first~~ began looking for a new site in 1965.

E.   The receipt will then be returned ~~back~~ to you.

22

The following letter is riddled with no less than 11 redundancies. Circle each one and cross out the unnecessary word or words.

~~Gentlemen~~ and Sirs:

We have ~~just~~ recently developed a ~~new and~~ original product which we plan to ~~introduce~~ ~~to the market~~ in late Spring ~~or early Summer~~. After much ~~thought and~~ deliberation, we have decided to launch an all-out, ~~no-holds-barred~~ advertising ~~and promotional~~ campaign to acquaint the public with our product before it comes out. As your firm has a reputation for being ~~both~~ reliable ~~and trustworthy~~, we would like to ~~sit down and~~ consult with you on ~~ways and means~~ of best marketing our product.

Cordially ~~and courteously~~ yours,

. . . .

Gentlemen ~~and Sirs~~:

We have ~~just~~ recently developed a new ~~and original~~ product which we plan to introduce to the market in late Spring ~~or early Summer.~~ After much thought ~~and deliberation,~~ we have decided to launch an all-out, ~~no-holds-barred~~ advertising ~~and promotional~~ campaign to acquaint the public with our product before it comes out. As your firm has a reputation for being ~~both~~ reliable ~~and trustworthy,~~ we would like to ~~sit down and~~ consult with you on ways ~~and means~~ of best marketing our product.

Cordially ~~and courteously~~ yours,

REVIEW

23

In this lesson you have learned how to delete unnecessary words, revise wordy phrases, and eliminate redundancies. The following sentence contains an example of each of these mistakes. Revise it.

~~Please be advised that~~ your order for 21 barrels of commercial grade oil
has been received ~~and duly noted~~ and _{/imeatate} shipment has been arranged ~~for~~
~~the immediate future.~~ (28 words)

· ·

~~Please be advised that~~ your order for 21 barrels of commercial grade oil

immediate
has been received ~~and duly noted~~ and ∧ shipment has been arranged ~~for~~
~~the immediate future.~~ (18 words, a saving of 10)

or

Immediate shipment of your order for 21 barrels of commercial grade oil

has been arranged. (15 words, a saving of 13)

or

We have arranged to ship your order for 21 barrels of commercial grade oil

immediately. (15 words, a saving of 13)

24

Each of the following sentences contains one or more verbosities. Revise them.

A.   ~~During the time that~~ *while* I am on vacation, my secretary, ~~whose name is~~ Mrs. Winters, will be in charge of petty cash.

B.   ~~Because of the fact of~~ *due to* recent discoveries, we shall have to begin our planning over ~~again~~.

C.   ~~As a consequence of this~~ *Therefore*, please let us hear from you ~~at an early~~ *soon* ~~date~~.

D.   ~~In the normal course~~ *Usually* ~~of procedure~~, we try to increase sales ~~in the neigh-borhood~~ of ~~about~~ five or six percent a year.

. . . .

     While, When

A.   ~~During the time that~~ I am on vacation, my secretary, ~~whose name is~~ Mrs. Winters, will be in charge of petty cash.

B.   Because of ~~the fact of~~ recent discoveries, we shall have to begin our planning over ~~again.~~

     Therefore, Consequently   soon

C.   ~~As a consequence of this~~, please let us hear from you ~~at an early date.~~

     Usually, Normally, Generally

D.   ~~In the normal course of procedure~~, we try to increase sales ~~in the neigh-borhood of~~ about five ~~or six~~ percent a year.

25a

Revise the following letter to make it more concise.

EMPIRE DECORATORS, INC.
1621 Broadway
New York, New York

February 16

Mr. Harold Phelps

Stasson & Phelps, Inc.

16 Spring Street

New York, New York

Dear Mr. Phelps:

~~It happens that~~ I have just ~~now~~ received your letter inviting our bid for ~~the purpose of~~ remodeling your offices ~~located~~ at 16 Spring Street. ~~As a consequence of this,~~ _Therefore_ our estimate is not based on a ~~full and~~ complete examination of the premises ~~as we would prefer in the normal course of procedure.~~ ~~For example,~~ although we have included a figure for painting costs for ~~the extent of~~ 1672 sq. ft. of wall area, we have not included a figure for any preliminary ~~or prerequisite~~ costs that may be involved in preparing the walls for painting ~~due to the fact that~~ _since_ their condition is an unknown factor.

However, in order ~~that you may~~ _to_ gain a more realistic picture of this matter, you may add ~~about~~ 10 or 12% to our bid to cover any additional ~~or extra~~ costs.

Respectfully,

EMPIRE DECORATORS, INC.
1621 Broadway
New York, New York

February 16

Mr. Harold Phelps

Stasson & Phelps, Inc.

16 Spring Street

New York, New York

Dear Mr. Phelps:

~~It happens that~~ I have just ~~now~~ received your letter inviting our bid for ~~the~~

Consequently
~~purpose of~~ remodeling your offices ~~located~~ at 16 Spring Street. ∧ ~~As a con-~~

~~sequence of this,~~ our estimate is not based on a ~~full and~~ complete examina-

normally
tion of the premises as we ∧ would prefer ~~in the normal course of procedure.~~

For example, although we have included a figure for painting costs for ~~the~~

~~extent of~~ 1672 sq. ft. of wall area, we have not included a figure for any

preliminary ~~or prerequisite~~ costs that may be involved in preparing the walls

as, because, since
for painting ~~due to the fact that~~ their condition is ~~an~~ unknown ~~factor.~~

to
However, ~~in order that you may~~ gain a more realistic picture ~~of this matter,~~

you may add ~~about~~ 10 or 12% to our bid to cover any additional ~~or extra~~

costs.

Respectfully,

25b

The letter should now read:

Dear Mr. Phelps:

I have just received your letter inviting our bid for remodeling your offices at 16 Spring Street. Consequently, our estimate is not based on a complete examination of the premises as we normally would prefer. For example, although we have included a figure for painting costs for 1672 sq. ft. of wall area, we have not included a figure for any preliminary costs that may be involved in preparing the walls for painting as their condition is unknown.

However, to gain a more realistic picture, you may add 10 or 12% to our bid to cover any additional costs.

As a reader, which of these two versions of the letter, the original or the revised, creates a better impression of the company? _____ *revised* _____

· ·

the revised version

This is the end of Lesson 1. Now turn to page 151 and take the Quiz for Lesson 1.

LESSON 2 | KEEPING YOUR READER'S INTEREST

Part I | SPECIFIC WORDS AND ACTIVE SENTENCES

Lesson 2 consists of two parts, each taking about an hour to complete. Part I will cover specific words and active sentences, and Part II will cover links and parallelism.

Specific Words: As mentioned in the Introduction, clarity is always a prerequisite for the business letter that best does the job for the writer and his firm. Thus, it is extremely important that you choose words that most exactly express your meaning. You may have a very clear and precise thought that you wish the reader to understand, but if you do not choose the right words to express it, the reader may misunderstand—with unpleasant consequences for yourself and your firm.

Generally, business writers have a tendency to use general words when *specific words* are needed. These general words are often clichés and are usually plugged in without too much thought. Below is a sentence containing two general words which should be replaced with more specific ones.

> Our production manager, Mr. Calhoun, feels that if your firm adopts the Merckle Computer System, it will have a *measurable effect* on production efficiency.

This sentence tells us very little because the writer has used two general words, "measurable effect." What does "measurable" really tell us? Will the effect on production efficiency be large, small, or something in between? All such effects are presumably "measurable." And what about "effect" itself? Will production be beneficially or detrimentally influenced by the computer system? These questions go unanswered because the two words are too general to convey anything but the vaguest of concepts.

Granted, the writer of the above sentence could make up for its lack of clarity in other sentences, but he would then probably be guilty of wordiness. For a sentence that is unclear is often inconcise.

The first part of the upcoming lesson will give you some practice in choosing specific words to make meaning clearer.

Active Sentences: The second part of the lesson will show you how to make your sentences active, that is, to write them so that the verb is in the active voice. If your letters contain many active sentences, they will not only be more concise but more lively and interesting. To demonstrate this point, we present below the first parts of two news articles—one with many active sentences and one with many passive sentences.

(Passive)
COLLISION REPORTED ON MAIN STREET

Shortly after 3 p.m. yesterday, at the intersection of Main and Farnum Streets, there was an accident between James P. O'Hara's late model convertible and a pickup truck, driven by Mr. A. C. Jones. A load of watermelons was being carried by the truck. These watermelons were deposited by the impact on the sidewalk in front of Dealy's Drugstore. A cry of "free watermelons!" was immediately set up by a small boy.

(Active)
CAR AND TRUCK COLLIDE ON MAIN STREET

Shortly after 3 p.m. yesterday, at the intersection of Main and Farnum Streets, Mr. James P. O'Hara's late model convertible collided with Mr. A. C. Jones' pickup truck. The impact deposited the truck's load of watermelons on the sidewalk in front of Dealy's Drugstore. A small boy immediately set up a cry of "free watermelons!"

The second paragraph is shorter and more lively primarily because all the sentences are active, while the first one has too many passive sentences.

SPECIFIC WORDS

1a

Suppose you are a regional sales manager of your firm, and you have recently instituted a successful incentive program for your salesmen. You are now writing to your boss to tell him about it. Which of the following sentences is most likely to arouse his interest? _____ least likely? ___A___

A.   The incentive program proved worthwhile.

B.   The incentive program was effective in raising sales.

C.   The incentive program raised sales by 40% in three weeks.

. . . .

C, A

1b

Which of the above sentences is the most specific? _____ the least? _____

. . . .

C, A

2a

Which of the following words is most specific? _____

    A.   communication

    B.   letter

    C.   message

    D.   thought

. . . .

    B.   letter

2b

Suppose you have received a complimentary letter from a customer and wish to acknowledge it. Fill in the best of the words A–D above in the following sentence:

I received your _____ today and wish to thank you for writing us about the additional uses you've found for our product.

. . . .

    letter

3a

Which of the following verbs is most specific? ___A___

   A.   to phone

   B.   to contact

   C.   to be (in touch with)

· ·

   A.   to phone

3b

Which of the following sentences is most informative? ___B___

   A.   I'll contact you on Tuesday.

   B.   I'll phone you Tuesday.

   C.   I'll be in touch with you Tuesday.

· ·

   B

4

   to send

   to forward

   to mail

Write in the most specific of the above three verbs in the following sentence:

   As you suggested, I will ___mail___ our Fall Catalogue to you as soon
   as we receive it from our printers.

· ·

   mail

5a

Cross out the uninformative, general word in the following sentence:

Dr. Small's lecture was ~~worthwhile.~~

. . . .

Dr. Small's lecture was ~~worthwhile.~~

5b

Of the following words, circle the *word or words* that are more specific than "worthwhile."

valuable

informative

good

witty

. . . .

valuable

(informative)

good

(witty)   (Dr. Small's lecture was witty, informative, enlightening,

stimulating, etc.)

6

In each of the following sentences cross out the vague word and write in something more specific.

             was mailed
   A. A copy of our report ~~went~~ to you this morning.
          phone
   B. Please ~~communicate~~ with us no later than Friday.
                            letter
   C. Please excuse the delay in answering your ~~message~~ but I just returned

      from vacation.

. . . .

                        was mailed, was sent by parcel post, etc.
   A. A copy of our report ~~went~~ to you this morning.

          call, write, etc.
   B. Please ~~communicate~~ with us no later than Friday.

                               letter, note, etc.
   C. Please excuse the delay in answering your ~~message~~ but I just returned

      from vacation.

SPECIFIC VERBS

7

In each of the following pairs of verbs, circle the more specific one.

. . . .

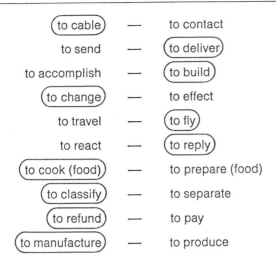

(to cable)	—	to contact
to send	—	(to deliver)
to accomplish	—	(to build)
(to change)	—	to effect
to travel	—	(to fly)
to react	—	(to reply)
(to cook (food))	—	to prepare (food)
(to classify)	—	to separate
(to refund)	—	to pay
(to manufacture)	—	to produce

8a

One of the best ways to invigorate your sentences is to use specific verbs. Sentences with specific verbs are not only clearer but more concise. For example, the following sentence has a general verb.

Mr. Jones *effected* a complete overhaul of the organization of the office.

This is not a very bad sentence, but it can be improved by using a more specific verb than "effected." Notice that the real action that Mr. Jones performed is hiding in the noun, "overhaul." If we convert this "action noun" to an "action verb" and substitute that verb for "effected," we come up with:

Mr. Jones completely *overhauled* the organization of the office.

This sentence is three words shorter and five times as vigorous as the first one.

Recovery of lost articles <u>can be accomplished </u>by applying at the manager's office.

Underline the verb in the above sentence.

. . . .

Recovery of lost articles <u>can be accomplished</u> by applying at the manager's office.

8b

(Recovery) of lost articles <u>can be accomplished</u> by applying at the manager's office.

Is this verb vague or specific? _specific_

. . . .

vague

8c

Now circle the word in the above sentence in which the action of the sentence is hiding.

. . . .

(Recovery) of lost articles <u>can be accomplished</u> by applying at the manager's office.

8d

Now rewrite this sentence by replacing the verb "accomplished" with a more specific one.

Lost articles can be _recovered_ by applying at the manager's office.

. . . .

recovered

9a

Underline the verb in the following sentence:

We <u>achieved</u> success in raising production.

. . . .

✓ We achieved (success) in (raising) production.

9b

Circle the word or words in which the action of this sentence is hidden.

· ·

✓ We achieved (success) in (raising) production.

9c

Now rewrite the sentence by filling in the verb.

We _*succeeded*_ in raising production.

· ·

✓ succeeded

9d

Rewrite the sentence by using the other action as the verb. *We*

successfully raised production

· ·

We successfully *raised* production.

10a

As shown in the previous frame, there are often several ways that an idea can be expressed. The way you express your ideas should always reflect your own style and personality. However, some faults should be avoided because they tend to make your writing less clear and concise.

Below are four sentences saying the same thing. Which one needs to be re-written? _____

   A. You can expect delivery of your order before Wednesday.

   B. Your order will be delivered before Wednesday.

   C. Delivery of your order will be effected before Wednesday.

   D. We will deliver your order before Wednesday.

· ·

   C. Delivery of your order <u>will be effected</u> before Wednesday.

10b

Using our answer above, cross out the verb and circle the word in which action is hiding.

· ·

   C. (Delivery) of your order ~~will be effected~~ before Wednesday.

10c

Rewritten, the sentence would now resemble sentence B above. However, could you have used sentences A, B, or D just as well? ___yes___

· ·

        yes

11a

In each of the following sentences, cross out the vague verb and circle the word in which the action is hidden.

A. A price increase on all replacement parts was effected last month.

B. We sustained a loss of almost $40,000 in yesterday's fire.

C. We suggest that automation of the 51st Street plant be accomplished during the slack summer months.

D. Registration of claims will be accepted at the offices of Harrison & Jones.

. . . .

A. A price ⟨increase⟩ on all replacement parts ~~was effected~~ last month.

B. We ~~sustained~~ a ⟨loss⟩ of almost $40,000 in yesterday's fire.

C. We suggest that ⟨automation⟩ of the 51st Street plant ~~be accomplished~~ during the slack summer months.

D. ⟨Registration⟩ of claims ~~will be accepted~~ at the offices of Harrison & Jones.

11b

Now rewrite each of the above sentences by filling in the verb:

A. Prices on all replacement parts _increased_ last month.

B. We _lost_ almost $40,000 in yesterday's fire.

C. We suggest that the 51st Street plant be _automated_ during the slack summer months.

D. Claims can be _registered_ at the offices of Harrison & Jones.

. . . .

A. increased, rose
B. lost
C. automated
D. registered

12

The following paragraph is a model of vague verbosity. To revise it, first cross out any vague words and then circle any words in which the action of a sentence is hiding. Then write in your corrections over the crossed out words.

In response to your ~~communication~~ *phone call* of the 19th, let me ~~first make known my~~ congratulations ~~on~~ *on your* your proposal ~~to achieve a~~ *to* streamlining ~~of our~~ *our* accounting department. The plan seems ~~both~~ worthwhile ~~and workable.~~ ~~I am of the opinion,~~ *I feel* therefore, that your plan should be introduced for consideration by our board at their next meeting, and I will ~~be in touch with~~ *phone* you when ~~they effect~~ a decision to adopt it ~~or not.~~ *has been reached*

. . . .

In response to your ~~communication~~ *letter, phone call, etc.* of the 19th, let me first ~~make known my~~ *congratulate you* (congratulations) on your proposal to ~~achieve a~~ (streamlining) *streamline* ~~of~~ our accounting department. The plan seems ~~both worthwhile and~~ workable. I ~~am of the~~ *think* (opinion,) therefore, that your plan should be ~~introduced for~~ (consideration) *considered* by our board at their next meeting, and I will ~~be in touch with~~ you when they ~~effect~~ *call, write, etc.* a (decision) *decide* to adopt it or not.

This paragraph should now read:

In response to your letter of the 19th, let me first congratulate you on your proposal to streamline our accounting department. The plan seems workable. I think, therefore, that your plan should be considered by our board at their next meeting, and I will call you when they decide to adopt it or not.

ACTIVE SENTENCES

13a

Jones wrote the letter.

In active sentences, the subject is the doer of the action. What word is the subject of the above sentence? _____*Jones*_____

. . . .

Jones

13b

The above sentence is (an active/a passive) sentence.

Circle your choice.

. . . .

an active sentence

(Because "Jones" is both the subject and the doer of the action, the above sentence is an active sentence; that is, its verb is in the active voice.)

13c

The letter was written by Jones.

What word is the subject of the above sentence? _____*letter*_____

. . . .

letter

13d

In the above sentence, the word "letter" is (the doer of the action/acted upon).

. . . .

acted upon

13e

Therefore, the above sentence is (an active/a passive) sentence.

· ·

a passive sentence

14a

A.   The report of preliminary findings was delivered by John Masters.

B.   We expect to publish our annual report in late June.

Underline the subjects of each of the above sentences.

· ·

A.   The <u>report</u> of preliminary findings was delivered by John Masters.

B.   We expect to publish our annual report in late June.

14b

Using our answer above, circle the doers of the action in each of the above sentences.

· ·

A.   The <u>report</u> of preliminary findings was delivered by John Masters.

B.   We expect to publish our annual report in late June.

14c

Which sentence is active, A or B? _____ B _____

· ·

B

15a

Circle the doer of the main action in each of the following sentences.

A. The turret lathe in the front row was repaired by (Peabody, Inc.)

✗ B. (It) is thought by some that our gold reserves are dangerously low.

C. (We) need to revamp our advertising program in time for next season.

✗ D. Nobody can foresee what (the stock market) will do these days.

E. A new discount rate will be announced by the (Federal Reserve Board) next month.

. . . .

A. The turret lathe in the front row was repaired by (Peabody, Inc.)

B. It is thought by (some) that our gold reserves are dangerously low.

C. (We) need to revamp our advertising program in time for next season.

D. (Nobody) can foresce what the stock market will do these days.

E. A new discount rate will be announced by the (Federal Reserve Board) next month.

15b

Which of the above sentences are active? _____C. D._____

. . . .

C and D

15c

Make the passive sentences above active by filling in the subject and verb in the following: *Peabody, Inc*   ~~*was*~~ *repared*

A. ____~~*John*~~____ ____~~*operated*~~____ the turret lathe in the

     SUBJECT   VERB

front row.

B. ____*Some*____ ____*thought*____ that our gold reserves

     SUBJECT   VERB

are dangerously low.

E. *the Federal Reserve Bd* *will announce* a new discount rate

     SUBJECT   VERB

next month.

. . . .

A. Peabody, Inc. _____   repaired _____

        SUBJECT   VERB

B. Some _____   think _____

        SUBJECT   VERB

E. The Federal Reserve Board will announce _____

        SUBJECT   VERB

(Notice how much shorter and more direct the active versions are.)

16a

A. The meeting came to order.

B. The case was closed.

In which sentence is the subject the doer of the action? ____*A*____

. . . .

A

16b

Which sentence is the active sentence? ___*A*___

. . . .

A

16c

Sentence B above is a passive sentence. Is the doer of the action present in the sentence? ___*No*___

. . . .

no

16d

Think up a plausible doer of the action and rewrite sentence B so that it is active.

___*John closed the case.*___

_____

. . . .

The police (the F.B.I., the investigator, etc.) closed the case.

_____

17a

As you can see from our last example, the doer of the action is not always present in the sentence. However, this will not be a problem in your own letters because you will of course know who or what is performing the action of the sentence. Suppose you have written the following:

A letter was received today from Nome, Alaska.

Is this sentence active or passive? ___*passive*___

. . . .

passive

17b

A letter was received today from Nome, Alaska.

Think up a doer of the action for the above sentence and make it active.

The company received a letter from Nome, Alaska today.

....

I (We, Mr. Jones, Someone, etc.) received a letter from Nome, Alaska today.

18a

Sometimes, a sentence is passive and its verb is too general. For example:

(Agreement) on the overtime-wage issue was reached last month by Local 201

of the Iron Workers Union and the management of Teco Corporation.

Circle the word in the above sentence in which specific action is hidden.

....

(Agreement) on the overtime-wage issue was reached last month by Local 201

of the Iron Workers Union and the management of Teco Corporation.

18b

Now revise the sentence by making it active and by using the specific action as

the verb. *Local 201 of the Iron workers Union ~~reached an agreement~~ and the management of Teco Corporation reached an agreement on the overtime-wage issue last month.*

Local 201 of the Iron Workers Union and the management of Teco Corporation agreed (reached an agreement) on the overtime-wage issue last month.

19a

Revise the following sentences so that they are active. If necessary, use a more specific verb and/or make up a plausible doer of the action.

A comprehensive report on marketing techniques has been prepared by Thomas Brown Associates.

Thomas Brown Associates prepared a comprehensive ~~mark~~ report on marketing techniques.

Thomas Brown Associates has prepared a comprehensive report on marketing techniques.

19b

An improved method of transporting our natural gas products is necessary to meet the increased demand in the suburbs.

This company must improve the method of transporting our natral gas products, to meet the increased demand in the suburbs.

We (Our firm, etc.) must improve our methods of transporting our natural gas products to meet the increased demand in the suburbs.

19c

A neutralization of the corrosive acids in the bottom of the mixing vat is accomplished by this new, white compound.

This new, white compound neutralizes the corresive acids in the bottom of the mixing vat.

. . . .

This new, white compound neutralizes the corrosive acids in the bottom of the mixing vat.

20

Below is a letter written by a paper products manufacturer in reply to a customer who has complained that some adding machine tape, which he bought from a local wholesaler, was damaged. He has asked the manufacturer to replace the order.

Revise this letter so that the sentences are active.

PARAGON PAPER PRODUCTS, INC.
16 Faraday Avenue

June 19

Mr. George E. Jackson
Office Supply Manager
Regent Insurance Company
11 Wilson Street

Dear Mr. Jackson:

My apology is rendered to you for the trouble you have had with your order for adding machine tape. However, it is my advice that a complaint be filed by you with your local wholesaler because it appears that the damage described by you was caused by his mishandling. Perhaps the carton containing the tape was inadvertently slashed by his stockboy. If so, the replacement of your order would have to be accomplished by the wholesaler.

However, if the name of your supplier is furnished us, an inquiry on your behalf will be gladly sent him from this office.

Sincerely,

Please Accept my apology for the trouble you have had with your order for adding machine tapes. I advise you to file a complaint with your local wholesaler, as it appears the damage described was caused by his mishandling. Perhaps the stockboy inadvertently stacked the cartons containing the tapes. ~~Therefore~~ If so, the wholesaler should accomplish ~~the replacement of your~~ ~~would be~~ the replacement. However, If you will furnish us with the name of your supplier, we will be glad to send an inquiry on your behalf.

Your revision of the above letter does not have to compare word for word with ours below. However, it should have a majority of active sentences.

Dear Mr. Jackson:

I apologize to you for the trouble you have had with your order for adding machine tape. However, *I advise* you to file a complaint with your local wholesaler because it appears that his *mishandling caused* the damage *you described.* Perhaps his *stockboy inadvertently slashed* the carton containing the tape. If so, your *wholesaler would have to replace* your order.

However, if *you will furnish* us with the name of your wholesaler, *we* (this office) *will gladly send* him an inquiry in your behalf.

Sincerely,

This is the end of Part I. Now turn to page 153 and take the Quiz for Part I.

Part II | **LINKS AND PARALLELISM**

Links: Links are words which serve the reader in much the same way as road signs serve the driver of a car. They tell him what to expect and thus make his trip safer and smoother. The first section of Part II will show you how to connect your ideas with links so that the relationships between them are clearly understood by the reader.

Parallelism: This is one of the most useful writing devices available to the writer of better business letters. When used correctly and appropriately, it can bring order and clarity to much of your writing. Thus, the second section of Part II will show you how to apply this writing device and how to avoid some of the more common errors associated with it.

LINKS

1a

The two most commonly used links are "and" and "but." "And" is a signal that says to the reader, "Here comes another idea," while "but" says, "Here comes a contrasting idea." When used correctly, these links can help your reader understand the relationships between your ideas.

    A.   Air freight is very fast.

    B.   It is expensive.

Sentence A above expresses (an advantage/a disadvantage) of air freight.

Sentence B expresses (an advantage/a disadvantage) of air freight.

. . . .

an advantage
a disadvantage

1b

A. Air freight is very fast.

B. It is expensive.

Therefore, Sentence B expresses (an additional／a contrasting) idea.

. . . .

a contrasting

1c

Fill in the appropriate link in the following:

Air freight is very fast, _____but_____ it is expensive.

. . . .

but

1d

Fill in the appropriate link in the following:

Air freight is very fast, _____and_____ it is convenient.

. . . .

and (The second idea is merely an additional idea. Thus, "and" is the appropriate link in this case.)

2

Fill in the appropriate links in the following:

A. The convention didn't generate any new ideas, _____but_____ we enjoyed the debate with the other delegates.

B. Our canning plant processes about 60 tons of crabs a day, _____and_____ the cans are then shipped to our Seattle warehouse for distribution.

C. We will arrive in Chicago on Tuesday, _and_ we will be staying at the Conrad Hilton.

D. We received your order for six cartons of X216 paper rolls, _but_ our inventory of X216 is temporarily depleted.

. . . .

A. but   B. and   C. and   D. but

The three links "or," "for," and "nor" are used in the following ways:

OR is used to link alternative ideas:

We expect Recon stock to climb ten points next month, *or* the bottom will drop out of it.

FOR is used when your second idea supports the first:

I didn't expect their stock to rise so soon, *for* it was dropping when I bought it.

NOR is used to link two negative ideas:

I didn't expect their stock to rise so soon, *nor* did I buy it for that reason.

Fill in the appropriate links in the following:

A. I know she is intelligent and efficient, _for_ she has worked with me for five years.

B. The tellers were not shown how to detect counterfeit currency, _nor_ were they told what to do with the phony bills when they did detect them.

C. You may sell your bonds _or_ convert them into shares of stock on a seven-for-one basis.

. . . .

A. for   B. nor   C. or

④

Draw a line from the link to the relationship it signals.

LINK   RELATIONSHIP

Indicates that the next idea will be:

and   a contrasting idea

but   a supporting idea

or   an additional idea

for   another negative idea

nor   an alternative idea

. . . .

and   a contrasting idea

but   a supporting idea

or   an additional idea

for   another negative idea

nor   an alternative idea

5

Fill in the appropriate link in each of the following:

A.   He is an efficient __and__ nervous worker.

B.   He is an efficient __and__ accurate worker.

C.   He is not an efficient worker __but__ is he accurate.

D.   He could be an efficient worker __and__ an accurate one, but not both.

E.   He can be a very efficient worker at times, __but__ I have seen him produce almost twice as many bottles as his fellow workers on a given day.

. . . .

A.   but   B.   and   C.   nor   D.   or   E.   for

6

On the left below is another set of links. Draw lines from the links to the relationships they signal.

LINK

RELATIONSHIP

Indicates that the next idea will be:

moreover
furthermore
also

a contrasting idea

however
nevertheless

a result of a previous idea or follow logically from a previous idea

consequently
therefore
hence
thus

an additional idea

· ·

moreover
furthermore
also

a contrasting idea

however
nevertheless

a result of a previous idea or follow logically from a previous idea

consequently
theretore
hence
thus

an additional idea

7

Draw lines from the links on the left to those on the right which have the same meaning.

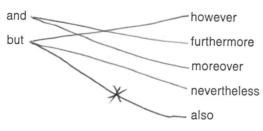

. . . .

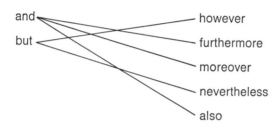

8a

Links like "and" and "but" are usually used to connect ideas *within* sentences, while links like "moreover" and "however" are usually used to connect ideas *between* sentences. For example:

The new product is definitely more effective than the old one, *but* it is more expensive.

The new product is definitely more effective than the old one. It is, *however,* more expensive.

Insert the appropriate link in the following:

The men worked ten-hour shifts around the clock for three weeks. *however,*

they were not able to finish the job by the deadline date of January 10th.

. . . .

However, Nevertheless

8b

Unlike links such as "and" and "but," which can be placed in only one position within a sentence, links such as "however" can be placed in several positions. However, since they are usually used to connect two sentences, they should be placed near the beginning of the second sentence.

Rewrite the second sentence above so that the link is near the beginning, but not at the beginning.

They were, however, not able to finish the job by the deadline date of January 10th.

They were not able, however, to finish the job by the deadline date of January 10th.

or

They were, however, not able to finish the job by the deadline date of January 10th.

(This second version is a little awkward. The first answer is preferable.)

9

THEREFORE is often used to indicate that the upcoming idea follows logically from the previous idea:

> Only employees with Top Secret security clearances are allowed access to the files in Vault A. Mr. Haines has only a Secret clearance. *Therefore,* Mr. Haines is not allowed access to the files in Vault A.

CONSEQUENTLY is often used to indicate that a result is upcoming:

> The elevators were not working yesterday morning. *Consequently,* many of our office personnel were late.

Both links, however, can be used interchangeably, as synonyms. So, when you have a clear case of logical deduction use "therefore," and when you have an obvious case of cause-effect, use "consequently." In other cases, let your instincts tell you which is better.

Insert the appropriate links in the following:

> In the past six months, there have been eleven serious car accidents at the Greens Point intersection. ~~There~~ *Consequently*, the city installed a traffic light last week.

> A meeting of the Executive Council has decided to award an extra week's vacation and a $500 bonus to all salesmen who surpass their quotas by 25% before July 16th. *Therefore*, Mr. Cable will be able to take his family to Lake Mead if he sells just ten more units next week.

. . . .

Consequently   Therefore

10

Fill in the appropriate links in the following:

> A. We will try to deliver your shipment by June 2 as you requested, *however* _____ we cannot guarantee delivery before June 15.
>
> B. We will deliver your shipment of men's suits by June 2. *However,* we will try to get the ladies' dresses to you within a week.

. . . .

A. but
(These two ideas could also be linked as follows: "We will try to deliver your shipment by June 2 as you requested; however, we cannot guarantee delivery before June 15.")

B. Moreover, Furthermore, Also
(This sentence could also be headed by "But" if the comma were not there.)

11

Fill in the appropriate links in the following:

A. This training program has been developed in consultation with experienced bankers _____and_____ has been thoroughly tested on bank employees.

B. This training program has been developed in consultation with experienced bankers. *Furthermore* it has been thoroughly tested on bank employees.

C. The weather bureau now predicts a late spring next year; *Therefore,* we can expect completion of the Rochester plant to be delayed at least a month.

D. I am increasingly alarmed by the drop-off in production at the Mercer Island factory. *Moreover,* I have learned through confidential sources that the union plans to strike us within two weeks.

E. Over the years, we have maintained a profit-sharing plan for those managers who show exceptional merit. Our competition, *however*, has not been able to lure our best people away from us.

F. This client usually pays for a purchase with cash __or__ by personal check.

G. I know the problems of that company as well as anybody, ___for___ I have been on its Board of Directors for the last ten years.

. . . .

A. and   B. Furthermore, Moreover, Also   C. Consequently, Therefore
D. Furthermore, Moreover, Also   E. consequently, therefore
F. or   G. for

12

Fill in the appropriate links in the following:

In order to coincide with the publication date, advertising promotion for your new cookbook will begin on August 10. *Consequently,* sales should be brisk until well into September, when they will probably fall off a bit. *However*, we do expect heavy sales during the Christmas season and will probably go into a second printing early next year. In fact, we may have to do this earlier if reviews are exceptionally good *or* if one of the book clubs decides to pick it up.

. . . .

Consequently, Therefore
However
or

13

Below is a paragraph in which necessary links have been omitted. Read it over first and then improve it by inserting appropriate links. You may edit and combine the sentences.

The paintings you asked for were crated; *however,* We shipped them via air-freight last Tuesday *and* ~~We~~ were not able to find your Aztec pottery in our Bleeker Street warehouse. A search of the files did not disclose any record, *Therefore,* ~~of it either~~. We have sent a letter of inquiry in your behalf to Mason Brothers Storage, Inc., since they may have kept the pottery after the World's Fair exhibition.

. . . .

                                and

The paintings you asked for were crated. ~~We~~ shipped ~~them~~ via air-freight last

          However, we

Tuesday. ~~We~~ were not able to find your Aztec pottery in our Bleeker Street

     , nor did a   Consequently, we

warehouse. ~~A~~ search of the files ~~did not~~ disclose any record of it ~~either.~~ ~~We~~

have sent a letter of inquiry in your behalf to Mason Brothers Storage, Inc.,

since they may have kept the pottery after the World's Fair exhibition.

PARALLELISM

14

Parallelism is a writing device which allows you to say to your reader, "Here are some ideas which have something in common and which I have arranged side by side in the same grammatical form." Parallelism allows you to bring symmetry and order to your writing.

All of the words, except one, in each of the groups below have something in common. Circle the discordant word in each group.

think	inventory	swiftly
consider	stock	slowly
ponder	merchandise	quickly
talk	invoice	rapidly

. . . .

think	inventory	swiftly
consider	stock	slowly
ponder	merchandise	quickly
talk	invoice	rapidly

15

In each of the following groups of words, one word doesn't have the same grammatical form as the others. Circle it.

thinking   inventory   swiftly

considered   stock   quick

pondered   merchandised   rapidly

· ·

thinking   inventory   swiftly

considered   stock   quick

pondered   merchandised   rapidly

16a

Ideas that have something in common are said to be parallel, as are words and groups of words that have the same grammatical form. Thus when you express parallel ideas in parallel grammatical forms, you are using the device of parallelism.

Below are two versions of the same thought. In which one are parallel ideas expressed in parallel forms? ___B___

A. The mail room receives incoming mail, which is then sorted, and an employee delivers it.

B. The mail room receives, sorts, and delivers all incoming mail.

· ·

B.

16b

Circle the parallel words in sentence B above.

· ·

B. The mail room receives, sorts, and delivers all incoming mail.

17a

Our company has a reputation for *high-quality work*, for *progressive management*, and for *being reliable.*

Do the above three italicized word groups express parallel ideas? _Yes_

. . . .

yes

17b

Are they expressed in parallel grammatical forms? _Yes_

. . . .

no

17c

Circle the phrase that is not parallel.

. . . .

Our company has a reputation for *high-quality work*, for *progressive management*, and for *being reliable.*

17d

Make this item parallel with the others by completing the following:

Our company has a reputation for high-quality work, for progressive management, and for _reliability_.

. . . .

reliability

18a

In which of the following sentences are parallel ideas expressed in parallel forms?

X B & C

A. We are not responsible for lost or stolen articles or any items that have been misplaced.

B. If we receive your order before June 10th, we can promise delivery by the end of the month.

C. If you will prepare the letter, our staff will address, stuff, and mail the envelopes.

. . . .

C

18b

Rewrite sentence A above so that it expresses its parallel ideas in parallel grammatical forms.

We are not responsible for
lost, stolen or misplaced
articles.

. . . .

We are not responsible for lost, stolen, or misplaced articles (items).

19

Parallel ideas may be expressed in:

1. parallel single words, or
2. parallel phrases, or
3. parallel clauses, or
4. parallel independent clauses.

Each of the following sentences contains one of the above parallel constructions. Write the number of each grammatical form after the sentence that exemplifies it.

A. We will consider locations in an office building, in an apartment house, or in a commercial loft. __2__

B. This stock tends to rise in the summer, and it tends to decline in the winter. __4__

C. The speech was monotonous, wordy, and vague. __1__

D. We are looking for applicants who are intelligent and who are willing to work hard. __3__

· ·

A. 2   B. 4   C. 1   D. 3

20a

After the clerk told us where to go, he then instructed us on what to do and also how to do it.

Circle the three parallel ideas in the sentence above.

· ·

After the clerk told us where to go, he then instructed us on what to do and also how to do it.

20b

After the clerk told us (where to go,) he then instructed us on (what to do) and also (how to do it.)

Now rewrite the sentence:

The clerk told us *where to go* , *what to do* , and *how to do it.*

. . . .

The clerk told us *where to go, what to do,* and *how to do it.*

21

After the lathes are crated at the factory, we then ship them from our warehouse.

Rewrite the above sentence so that it expresses its parallel ideas in parallel grammatical forms.

_____

_____

. . . .

We crate the lathes at the factory and ship them from our warehouse. (active)

or

The lathes are crated at the factory and shipped from our warehouse. (passive)

22

This computer is fast, accurate, and can be programmed easily.

Rewrite the above sentence so that it expresses its parallel ideas in parallel grammatical forms.

This computer is fast accurate, and can be easily programed.

. . . .

This computer is fast, accurate, and easy to program.

or

This computer is fast, accurate, and easily programmed.

23a

. . . either . . . or . . .

. . . neither . . . nor . . .

. . . not only . . . but also . . .

These sets of words, called "correlatives," are used to join parallel ideas. They should always be followed by grammatical forms that are identical. For example:

Mr. Hayes will allow Jones either *to go* to the San Francisco Conference or *to meet* Mr. Townes at our office, but not both.

Note that the grammatical constructions immediately following "either" and "or" are identical, as they should be.

Now look at the following:

We hoped *not only* to obtain realistic production estimates from the new management group *but also* a summary of raw-material needs was aimed at.

Are the grammatical forms following each of the correlatives identical? *No*

. . . .

no

23b

Rewrite the above sentences so that the forms following the two correlatives are parallel.

We hoped not only to obtain
realistic production estimates
from the new management group
but also to summarize
raw material needs

We hoped not only *to obtain* realistic production estimates from the new management group but also *to summarize* raw material needs.

24

Mr. Thomas was neither willing to learn nor did he have the ability to accept criticism.

Rewrite the above sentence so that the grammatical forms following "neither" and "nor" are parallel.

Mr. Thomas was neither willing to learn not was he able to accept criticism.

Mr. Thomas was neither *willing* to learn nor *able* to accept criticism.

or

Mr. Thomas was willing neither *to learn* nor *to accept* criticism.

(Note that these two versions have slightly different meanings.)

25a

Which of the following sentences exemplify the correct use of parallelism? _A.&E_

   A. ✓ In September, the inventory of Allied Flour Mills increases as it purchases the summer wheat harvest; and in November, its inventory decreases as it sells flour to its customers.

   B. ✗ The stock market remained steady on Wednesday, rose slightly on Thursday, and ~~was observed to drop~~ *dropped* sharply on Friday.

   C. ✗ Our employment office will be open Tuesday to accept applications and ~~for~~ *preform* interviews.

   D. ✗ The newly hired salesmen are trained, given sample cases, assigned territories, and ~~then we let them~~ *are sent out* out on their own.

   E. ✓ Tom not only attended the sales meeting but delivered a pep talk.

· ·

   A and E

25b

Cross out the parts of sentences B, C, and D that need reworking and insert your revision.

· ·

   B.   The stock market remained steady on Wednesday, rose slightly on Thursday, and ~~was observed to drop~~ *dropped* sharply on Friday.

   C.   Our employment office will be open Tuesday to accept applications and ~~for~~ interviews. *to conduct, hold, give, etc.*

   or

   Our employment office will be open Tuesday ~~to accept~~ *for* applications and for interviews.

   D.   The newly hired salesmen are trained, given sample cases, assigned territories, and then ~~we~~ let ~~them~~ out on their own.

26

The following paragraph can be improved by a more intelligent application of the principle of parallelism. Write in your revisions so that parallel ideas are expressed in parallel forms.

> I received your proposal for the development of training materials, and ~~it has~~ *I have* ~~been~~ forwarded ~~by me~~ *it* to our Executive Board for their consideration. With it, I included not only my own evaluation of your general plan of operation but ~~gave~~ + my opinion as to the accuracy of your cost estimates. Needless to say, I enthusiastically endorsed both parts as being realistic and ~~they are~~ carefully thought out.

. . . .

> I received your proposal for the development of training materials, and ~~it has been forwarded by me~~ *forwarded it* ʌ to our Executive Board for their consideration. With it, I included not only my own evaluation of your general plan of operation but + ~~gave~~ my opinion as to the accuracy of your cost estimates. Needless to say, I enthusiastically endorsed both parts as being realistic and ~~they are~~ carefully thought out.

Another way to revise the second sentence is as follows:

> With it, I included ~~not only~~ my own evaluation *not only* ʌ of your general plan of operation but ~~I gave my opinion as to~~ *of* ʌ the accuracy of your cost estimates.

This is the end of Part II. Now turn to page 157 and take the Quiz for Part II.

LESSON 3 | BEING NATURAL, COURTEOUS, AND PERSONAL

This lesson will help you achieve a natural, courteous, and personal style in your business letters. For it is just as important that your letters have these qualities as it is that they be clear and concise. Think for a moment about the way people speak to and interact with each other in business. Have you noticed that the ones who are most successful and effective usually are able to express themselves in a simple, unaffected manner? They are able, somehow, to give the impression that they are courteous and considerate—that they *care* about the people around them—while at the same time concentrating on the business at hand. However, it is the stuffed shirts and the loudmouths who are usually the butt of office jokes.

Isn't it logical to conclude that the style which most succeeds in the office is also the style that can best work in business letters? This may seem obvious, but unfortunately, some of the most fluent and effective business people become cold, pompous jargoneers when they write a letter. They feel that they have to fit their natural conversational mode of expression into a rigid mold called "the business writing style." For example, below is a letter written by an insurance adjuster to a customer who has had a car accident and has applied for damage benefits.

July 20

Dear Mrs. Harding:

Please be advised that the letter under date of June 6 would have been answered at a prior date to the present, if it had not been the case that it was addressed to the wrong department. Hereinafter, kindly address all correspondence in reference to your claim for damage benefits to the Automobile Liability Claims Division.

You claim that three individuals were witness to the alleged accident. However, this office cannot undertake consideration of the claim until such time as the names and addresses of these individuals are furnished us.

Sincerely,

This letter would probably inspire the reader with all the kindly instincts of a chicken hawk. It is pompous, rude, and cold primarily because of four basic faults. First, it contains archaic expressions such as "under date" and "hereinafter." This kind of wording was popular in business at the turn of the century, but since most firms do not want to appear old-fashioned, you would do well to eliminate all archaic expressions from your letters.

Second, the above letter contains many examples of inflated writing. This fault occurs because the writer chooses to use long, complex words when short, simple ones would serve just as well. Notice that the above writer has used expressions such as "a prior date" and "with reference to" when "sooner" and "about" would serve better.

This tendency to use inflated words stems from a slightly dishonest impulse that most letter writers experience when they find that they have something fairly simple and ordinary to say. So, to avoid the implication that *they* are simple and ordinary, they dress their words up to suggest a formality that is not strictly truthful. It is such impulses that lead us to write, "A thorough investigation was made as to the subject's whereabouts," instead of "I looked up his address in the telephone book."

The "Armed Forces Management" magazine touched on the subject of inflated writing in the following way:

INSTANT EXPERTISE*

A new aid for preparing speeches, briefings, etc. is circulating in the Defense Department in Ottawa. The "Buzzphrase Generator" gives instant expertise on matters pertaining to defense. Here it is:

COLUMN 1	COLUMN 2	COLUMN 3
0 integrated	0 management	0 options
1 total	1 organizational	1 flexibility
2 systematized	2 monitored	2 capability
3 parallel	3 reciprocal	3 mobility
4 functional	4 digital	4 programming
5 responsive	5 logistical	5 concept
6 optimal	6 transitional	6 time-phase
7 synchronized	7 incremental	7 projection
8 compatible	8 third-generation	8 hardware
9 balanced	9 policy	9 contingency

The procedure is simple. Think of any three-digit number. Select the corresponding buzzword from each column. Put them together and WHAM! POW! ZAP! You sound just like you know what you're talking about.

For instance, take the number 257. You get "systematized logistical projection." Would you prefer 349 (parallel digital contingency) or 935 (balanced reciprocal concept)? You don't know what it means, but don't worry, neither do "they." The important result is that the user now has the perfect aid for preparing any communication on the subject of national defense.

A third fault of the above letter is that it has too many negative thoughts and words. Note that the first sentence makes it abundantly clear to the reader that he has made a grievous error by sending his letter to the "wrong department." Certainly the reader, who happens to be a customer of the company, made a mistake. But why rub it in? The second sentence adds further offense by summarily ordering the customer to use the right address from here on. In the third sentence, the words "claim" and "alleged" imply that the reader may be lying about the witnesses and even about the accident itself. And the last sentence is again full of negative words.

* Reprinted from *Armed Forces Management,* June 1966.

The fourth fault is that the letter is too impersonal. Note that the writer avoids mention of himself or his firm most of the time by using the passive voice, and when he does refer to his firm, he calls it "this office."

This lesson will help you avoid these faults by encouraging you to write in a simple conversational style, to be courteous and positive, and to be personal by using a liberal sprinkling of words such as "I," "you," and "we." Thus, we hope you will write letters, not like the one above, but like the one below.

Dear Mrs. Harding:

I would have answered your letter of June 6 sooner, but it has just been forwarded to me from our Actuarial Department. I assure you that you will receive much more efficient service from us if you will address all future letters concerning your claim for automobile damage benefits to me, care of the Automobile Liability Claims Division.

In your letter, you said that three people witnessed the accident. May I have the names and addresses of these witnesses? As soon as I receive them, we will be happy to give prompt consideration to your claim.

Sincerely,

INFLATED WORDS

1

Below are a list of inflated phrases and a list of simple ones that mean exactly the same thing. Match them by drawing a line from each inflated phrase to its simple replacement.

INFLATED

SIMPLE

we deem it advisable

with reference to

I regret to inform you that

as requested by you

I am sorry that

we suggest

as you asked

about

· ·

we deem it advisable

with reference to

I regret to inform you that

as requested by you

I am sorry that

we suggest

as you asked

about

2a After
When your arive

~~Subsequent to your arrival~~, we will meet to discuss the program in Conference

Room A.

Cross out the inflated phrase in the above sentence.

· ·

~~Subsequent to your arrival~~, we will meet to discuss the program in Conference

Room A.

2b

Now write a deflated version of this phrase over the crossed-out portion in our

answer above.

· ·

After you arrive
~~Subsequent to your arrival,~~ we will meet to discuss the program in Conference

Room A.

3

Cross out the inflated phrase in the following sentence and write in a simpler version.

before you leave
I will call you ~~prior to your departure~~.

· ·

before you leave
I will call you ~~prior to your departure.~~

4

Cross out the inflated words in each of the following sentences and write in a simpler version.

I am sorry that
A. ~~I regret to inform you that~~ your contest entry arrived after the closing date.

about
B. I am writing ~~with reference to~~ your order #SA6201 which we sent out
after
~~subsequent to~~ your cancellation order.

We suggest
C. ~~It is deemed advisable~~ that all production of X692 be stopped until you

discover the source of the leak.
you requested
D. We have sent your order by rail as ~~requested by you~~.

· ·

A. ~~I regret to inform you that~~ your contest entry arrived after the closing date.
         I am sorry but

B. I am writing ~~with reference to~~ your order #SA6201 which we sent out
         about
~~subsequent to~~ your cancellation order.
    after

C. ~~It is deemed advisable~~ that all production of X692 be stopped until you
        We, I suggest, think
discover the source of the leak.

D. We have sent your order by rail as ~~requested by you.~~
         you asked

5

The following sentence is abominably inflated. Rewrite it.

I consider it advisable that you initiate a chemical analyzation of the foreign material at once.

I suggest that you initiate a chemical analyzation of the foreign material at once.

I suggest that you chemically analyze the foreign material at once.

6

Deflate the following letter by crossing out any inflated language and writing your revision over it. You may want to revise whole sentences since several are very wordy—another characteristic of inflated writing.

CENTROFLUX, INC.
"Your Neighborhood Appliance Center"
11 Greenwood Avenue
Portland, Oregon

Mrs. T. E. Waterman
15 Emery Place
Portland, Oregon

Dear Mrs. Waterman:

I reget
~~It is regrettable~~ to have to inform you that we cannot replace your washing
you asked
machine as ~~requested by you~~ in your letter of May 19th, since the breakdown
after
occurred ~~subsequent to~~ the expiration of the guaranty. However, I have been
if
informed that ~~in the event that~~ your washer undergoes repair at one of our
to
service centers, the cost ~~that will be incurred~~ by you will be only for ~~the~~ labor
~~of those individuals involved in such labor.~~

. . . .

Dear Mr. Waterman:

   I am sorry but
~~It is regrettable to have to inform you that~~ we cannot replace your washing

   you asked
machine as ~~requested by you~~ in your letter of May 19th, since the breakdown

   after the guaranty expired.   if
occurred ~~subsequent to the expiration of the guaranty.~~ However, ~~I have been~~

         is repaired
~~informed that in the event that~~ your washer ~~undergoes repair~~ at one of our

     to
service centers, the cost ~~that will be incurred by~~ you will be only for ~~the~~ labor

~~of those individuals involved in such labor.~~

The letter should now read something like this:

Dear Mrs. Waterman:

I am sorry but we cannot replace your washing machine as you asked in your letter of May 19th, since the breakdown occurred after the guaranty expired. However, if your washer is repaired at one of our service centers, the cost to you will be only for labor.

ARCHAIC EXPRESSIONS

7a

Archaic expressions, like inflated language, can hamper the tone of your letters. For example:

Pursuant to our agreement, I am enclosing a sight draft for $12,000.

Circle the archaic expression in the above sentence.

. . . .

(Pursuant to our agreement,) I am enclosing a sight draft for $12,000.

7b

A more natural substitution for this archaic phrase is "As we agreed." Another pet phrase of the ancients is "as per." Cross out this archaic expression in the following sentence and write in your revision.

                    we discussed
As ~~per our discussion~~, I have arranged a meeting with the Pedicone group for

next Tuesday.

. . . .

As we discussed, agreed,
~~As per our discussion~~, I have arranged a meeting with the Pedicone group for

next Tuesday.

7c

As per your letter of April 9th, we are enclosing two copies of our application form.

"As per" in the above sentence probably means "as you requested." What does it mean in the following?
as you advised

As per your suggestion in your letter of May 14th, I think we should by all means give a raise to the top three salesmen of each division.

. . . .

As you suggested

8

Write a simple substitute over each of the archaic phrases crossed out below.

A. ~~Enclosed herewith find~~ *Enclosed please find* six copies of the sales report for distribution to your salesmen.

B. I have ~~duly noted~~ *reviewed* your letter of January 9th and agree wholeheartedly with your conclusions.

. . . .

A. Here are, Enclosed are

B. read

9

Cross out the archaic phrases in the following paragraph and write your corrections over them.

As you requested in
~~As per your request~~ letter of March 10th, we will deliver a dictaphone to your
As we agreeded enclosed are
main office on Monday. And ~~pursuant to our arrangement, you will herewith find~~
read
is an installment-loan contract, which you should ~~duly note~~ and then ~~affix your~~

signa~~ture~~.

. . . .

As you requested in
~~As per~~ your ~~request~~ letter of March 10th, we will deliver a dictaphone to your
∧

                                as we arranged,   here is, I am enclosing, etc.
main office on Monday. And ~~pursuant to our arrangement, you will herewith find~~

                                      read   sign.
an installment-loan contract, which you should ~~duly note~~ and then ~~affix your~~

~~signature.~~

This paragraph should now read something like this:

As you requested in your letter of March 10th, we will deliver a dictaphone to your main office on Monday. And as we arranged, here is an installment-loan contract, which you should read and then sign.

POSITIVE AND NEGATIVE WORDS

10

Words not only have a dictionary meaning but an emotional meaning. Thus, when most of us read or hear words like "truth," "efficiency," "thank you," "improve," or "beauty," we tend to react pleasantly or positively. And when we are exposed to words like "arrogant," "you cannot," "pest," or "childish," our reactions usually are unpleasant or negative. However, some words, such as "fork," "mercantile," "policy," "smooth," or "travel," do not have much emotional meaning and thus they usually have a neutral effect on most of us.

Since a large majority of business letters are written to convey neutral facts and ideas, most of your letters will have a high proportion of neutral words. But you should realize that even the most ordinary or routine letter carries certain emotional overtones, either positive or negative. This ingredient becomes of primary importance when you are writing letters which convey thoughts and facts that can affect the reader's emotions. For example, a letter turning down an application for credit or employment has a high potential for doing great damage to the reader's feelings. In such letters, it is extremely important that the words you use are as neutral or positive as you can make them.

Below are three groups of words which more or less have the same dictionary meaning. In each group is a positive word, a negative word, and a neutral word. Put a plus (+) next to the positive words, a minus (−) next to the negative ones, and a zero (0) next to the neutral ones.

✕ limousine	_0_	✕ cautious	_−_	Hitler	_−_
automobile	_0_	prudent	_+_	✕ leader	_+_
pile of junk	_−_	cowardly	_−_	Abraham Lincoln	_+_

. . . .

limousine	+	cautious	0	Hitler	−
automobile	0	prudent	+	leader	0
pile of junk	−	cowardly	−	Abraham Lincoln	+

11 ✓/

Do the same thing for the following list of words:

punctual	—	worry	—
book	0	unfair	—
pen	0	loyalty	+
genuine	+	tardy	—
You must go to . . .	—	Please send us . . .	+
It is impossible to . . .	—	I appreciate . . .	+
✗because	—	incorrect	—

. . . .

punctual	+	worry	—
book	0	unfair	—
pen	0	loyalty	+
genuine	+	tardy	—
You must go to . . .	—	Please send us . . .	+
It is impossible to . . .		I appreciate . . .	I
because	0	incorrect	—

12a

I have fo✗und out that you are (delinquent) for three installment-loan payments. Circle the negative word or words that make this unnecessarily offensive.

. . . . *learned* . . . . *behind* . . . .

I (have found out) that you are (delinquent) for three installment-loan payments.

12b

Replace the negative words in our answer above with positive or neutral words if possible or with less negative words at least.

. . . .

notice, see, etc.   late in making, overdue on, behind on, etc.
I (have found out) that you are (delinquent) for three installment-loan payments.

13

No one enjoys being ordered about, whereas most of us react favorably to being asked.

Which of the following two sentences is most likely to get a favorable response?

A.   Payment of this invoice must reach our office by October 31st.
B.   May we have your payment by October 31st?

· ·

B

14

Change the following sentence to a more courteous request:

A prompt reply would be appreciated.

We would appreciate a reply as soon as possible.

· ·

May we hear from you soon?

or

Please reply as soon as possible.

15

Many times we emphasize the negative side of things rather than the positive. For instance:

Our office does not open until 9:45 a.m.

Doesn't the following say the same thing, but more positively?

Our office opens at 9:45 a.m.

Change the following sentence to emphasize the positive:

X Our office ~~is closed after~~ *closes at* 5:15 p.m.

. . . .

Our office is ~~closed after~~ open until 5:15 p.m.

16

We cannot deliver your shipment before next week.

Why tell the reader what you cannot do when you can just as easily tell him what you can do? Why not say:

We will be happy to deliver your shipment next week at the latest.

Revise the following sentence so that it tells the reader what *can* be done:

Because our next board meeting is not scheduled until January 13th, we will not be able to consider your proposal until then.

We will consider your proposal after our next board meeting on January 13th.

. . . .

We will be glad to consider your proposal at our next board meeting on January 13th.

17

Sometimes, of course, the thought you are trying to express is necessarily negative—as, for instance, when you must refuse a request. However, you can soften the
negative tone by eliminating any arrogant or condescending overtones.

> As you would know if you read our guaranty carefully, we do not repair
> damage caused by customer negligence.

Your reader may be at fault, but why not say,

> I am sorry that we cannot grant your request but our guaranty only covers the
> cost of replacing defective parts.

Revise the offensiveness out of the following sentence:

> Your application for this job has been denied since we specifically stated at
> the time you applied that we would only consider college graduates.

I am sorry that your application for this job has been denied, as we can only consider college graduates

> Because we are specifically looking for a college graduate, I am sorry we
> cannot consider your application for this job.

18

We are returning your loan application because you forgot to sign it. Therefore, we cannot process this form until you sign it in the space in the lower left-hand corner, which is clearly marked for this purpose, and return it promptly.

Revise this to make it more courteous and positive. You may cut out some parts of it.

In order that we may process
your loan application, we request
~~continue~~
that it be signed as ~~the~~ _indicated_
in the lower left-hand
corner. and returned to us

We will be glad to process your loan application as soon as you sign it in the lower left-hand corner and return it to us.

19

The following letter is designed to antagonize the reader. Rewrite it.

CENTRAL ELECTRIC COMPANY
118 Liberty Street
Tucson, Arizona

December 15

Mr. George Harding
11 Maiden Lane
Tucson, Arizona

Dear Mr. Harding:

This office has no record of any check received for your October payment as you claim. Therefore, unless you can furnish proof that you actually paid this bill, we will be forced to consider terminating your electrical service.

As we have no record of receiving your check for october, please furnish us with a copy of your cancelled check that we may research farther.

. . . .

Dear Mr. Harding:

I am sorry but we cannot find any record of your October payment. Could you therefore send us a photostat of your canceled check so that we can correct our files?

20

Rewrite the following letter so that it is both positive and friendly:

BROADWAY THEATRE AGENCY
135 West 45th Street
New York, New York

January 10

Dear Sir:

We have no orchestra seats available for HELLO DOLLY! on February 1st nor will we have any until March 1st. Also, balcony seats are sold out through March 1st. A check must accompany each order. Promptness is recommended.

The preformance of Hello Dolly on 2/1, however we will have has sold out seat available after 3/1. Please sent us your check with each order.

. . . .

Dear Sir:

I am sorry that we cannot fill your request for orchestra seats for HELLO DOLLY! on February 1st. However, both orchestra and balcony seats are available after March 1st.

May we have your check with your order soon?

THE PERSONAL TOUCH

21a

Many business writers must write letters that deal with the same problems over and over. Naturally, they tend to forget that their readers are individuals and that each one's problem is a little different from the next. However, the writer of more effective business letters does not forget. He makes a conscious effort to think of his reader as a person. Even a form letter that is sent to thousands of people can have the personal touch.

Which of the following paragraphs from a form letter is more personal? _____

    A.   Our new computer seems to have run amuck this week and added three extra 000's to all our checks. If you have been one of the astonished recipients of such a check, please return it to us and we will send you one for the correct amount at once.

    B.   A flaw in the electronic computer has resulted in the addition of an extra three zeros to all checks issued this week. If such a check has been received, it would be much appreciated if it were returned at once and a replacement with the correct amount will be issued.

. . . .

    A

21b

The first paragraph is more personal because it has several "you's" and "we's."

How many "you's" and "we's" are in the second? *none*

. . . .

    none

22

One of the best ways to make your letters personal is to sprinkle them liberally with "I," "you," and "we." Use "I" when you are speaking for yourself. Use "we" when you are speaking for a group within your organization or for the organization itself. Don't use "we" in such expressions as "we are sorry that you did not receive courteous service at our candy counter," since "we" in this case refers to the firm, and it is somewhat insincere to imply that the firm is "sorry." Instead, use "I" in such cases.

Rewrite the following sentence so that it is more personal:

It is assured that the deadline will be met by this firm.

I assure you that we will meet the deadline.

. . . .

I assure you that we will meet the deadline.

or

You can be sure that we will meet the deadline.

23

It is felt that your cost estimates should be reviewed by this writer before they are presented to Mr. Hanes.

Rewrite the above so it is more personal.

I~~tle~~ felt that your cost estimates should be reviewed by me, before ʸʰᵉʸ presented to Mr. Hanes

I feel (think) that I should review your cost estimates before you present them to Mr. Hanes.

or

I feel (think) that I should review your cost estimates before Mr. Hanes sees them.

24

Write in the appropriate pronoun in each of the following:

A. The editors and I have read your manuscript and ___*We*___ like it.

B. ___*We*___ require an average of 10 tons of rolled steel per month.

C. ___*I*___ will call you next week regarding my decision.

D. ___*I*___ am/~~are~~ sorry you have had bad luck with our blender.

E. Due to the recent strikes, ___*We*___ have been running late on deliveries this month.

· ·

A. we   B. we   C. I   D. I am   E. we

25

Cross out any pronouns that are incorrect or impersonal and write your revisions over them.

We are glad to hear ~~from anyone who~~ *that you* tried our coffee and liked it. True, ~~the~~ *our* price is a little higher than that of other blends—but then, ~~the~~ *We* blend ~~this firm uses~~ *you will* is of higher quality and ~~people~~ usually find that ~~they~~ *you* can use a smaller amount of our coffee to make more cups.

· ·

I am
~~We are~~ glad to hear ~~from anyone who~~ *that you* tried our coffee and liked it. True, ~~the~~ *our*

price is a little higher than that of other blends—but then, ~~the~~ *our* blend ~~this firm~~

you will *you*
~~uses~~ is of higher quality and ~~people~~ usually find that ~~they~~ can use a smaller

amount of our coffee to make more cups.

26

Sometimes the business writer, in his effort to insert "I," "you," and "we," will use too much "I" and "we." In other words, he talks too much about himself and his organization. However, readers are primarily interested in themselves and like to see a lot of "you's."

> I'm always glad to receive a letter from one of our customers who is satisfied
>
> with our Jet Beam Flashlight.

The reader probably is not interested in how the writer feels. Rewrite this by putting the emphasis on "you."

I ~~am always~~ was glad to receive your letter stating that you are satisfied with our Jet Beam Flashlight.

> Thank you for your letter indicating your satisfaction with your Jet Beam Flashlight.
>
> or
>
> I'm glad to hear that you are satisfied with your Jet Beam Flashlight.

27

Cross out the words in the following sentence that make it too self-centered and insert your revisions over them.

> I'm sorry to learn that ~~anyone is~~ *you are* dissatisfied with ~~our~~ *your* new Fluff-Dry Hairdryer.

. . . .

>   you are   your
>
> I'm sorry to learn that ~~anyone is~~ dissatisfied with ~~our~~ new Fluff-Dry Hairdryer.

28

I was glad to hear of your appointment to Chief of the Paris Bureau.

Why emphasize how your reader's appointment made you feel? Wouldn't it be more to the point to simply congratulate him?

Congratulations on
~~I was glad to hear of~~ your appointment to Chief of the Paris Bureau.

Now do the same for the following sentence:

~~I'm glad to hear of~~ your decision to stay on and help us out with the Stone-Paine project. *is welcomed*

. . . .

Thanks for deciding
~~I'm glad to hear of your decision~~ to stay on and help us out with the Stone-Paine project.

29

We offer two medical plans: one for individuals only and one that can include members of their immediate family.

The above sentence not only is addressed to a statistic but it also emphasizes what you do rather than what the reader can do. Rewrite it.

You may choose one of two medical plans, an individual or family plan.

. . . .

You can take out a medical plan for yourself only or one that can include your wife and children.

REVIEW

30

In this lesson you have learned about deflating inflated language, updating archaic expressions, eliminating negative overtones, and making your letters personal.

Each of the following sentences contains one or more faults. Cross them out and write your corrections over them.

A. ~~As per your order for~~ *Regarding your order of* 21 bales of cotton, we can~~not~~ deliver them ~~before~~ *after*

August 6th.

B. ~~It is deemed advisable~~ *We* ~~suggest~~ *are advised* by ~~those in this~~ *our* office that your short-term debt should be decreased by ~~the~~ *the* issuance of debentures in the amount of $1,000,000.

C. *your* Orders for additional fur pieces must reach ~~this office prior to~~ *us before* June 10th.

D. I was glad to find your report as excellent as I expected ~~it to be~~.

E. ~~As requested in your~~ *you As requested in your* letter of November 25th, an application for credit is ~~herewith~~ enclosed.

· ·

A. ~~As per~~ *Regarding, As for* your order for 21 bales of cotton, we can~~not~~ deliver them ~~before~~ *after*

August 6th.

or

We can deliver your order for 21 bales of cotton after August 6th.

B. ~~It is deemed advisable by those in this office~~ *We think, We feel* that your short-term debt *you should decrease*

~~should be decreased~~ by ~~the issuance of~~ *issuing* debentures ~~in the amount of~~ *for, worth*

$1,000,000.

C. *Please send your, May we have your* Orders for additional fur pieces ~~must reach this office prior to~~ *before* June 10th.

or

If you want additional fur pieces, please send your orders before June 10th.

(cont.)

D. ~~I was glad to find your report as~~ excellent ~~as I expected it to be.~~

Congratulations on your *report*

E. As ~~requested~~ *you asked* in your letter of November 25th, an application for credit ~~is~~ ~~herewith enclosed.~~ *here is, I am enclosing*

31

Revise the following letter so that it is natural, courteous, and personal.

CASE PHARMACEUTICALS, INC.

118 South Street

Newport News, Virginia

March 12

Mr. Donald Koosis

Proprietor

Church Hill Drug Store

Sato, Montana

Dear Mr. Koosis:

We have ~~at hand~~ *received* your letter ~~under date of~~ *dated* March 9th and have ~~duly~~ noted ~~the~~ *your* suggestion ~~that~~ we initiate extensive testing of our sedative, KLORSEL, because ~~you claim~~ it has painful side effects. However, ~~let me hasten to make~~ *please be* assur-anced that prior to ~~any~~ *our* drug being released on the market, ~~this firm~~ *we* submits it to a rigorous testing procedure, using both laboratory animals and selected groups of volunteers.

~~The opinion,~~ therefore, ~~is held by~~ our research and testing staff ~~that your so-called "deleterious side effects"~~ *believe these side effects* are due to causes other than KLORSEL. Sub-stantial evidence to the contrary is required before we could take such a sug-gestion into serious consideration.

We have rec'd your letter of 3/9 and have noted your suggestion that we initial extensive testing of our sedative, KLORSEL, because it has painful side effects.

. . . .

Dear Mr. Koosis:

I have carefully read your letter of March 9th, suggesting that we start extensive testing of our sedative, KLORSEL, because of the side effects. However, let me assure you that before we release any of our products on the market, we test them rigorously on both laboratory animals and selected groups of volunteers.

Could it possibly be, Mr. Koosis, that the side effects you describe are due to a cause other than KLORSEL? If you will send evidence of your suspicions, we will certainly give it serious consideration.

This is the end of Lesson 3. Now turn to page 159 and take the Quiz for Lesson 3.

LESSON 4 | THE START AND THE FINISH

The starting sentence of a business letter is one of the most important parts because it makes the first impression on the reader—for good or ill. For this reason, we spend the first half of this lesson teaching some of the better ways to start a business letter.

The second half covers some of the more effective ways of closing a business letter. Because the finish is usually the most memorable part of the letter, it offers the writer a unique opportunity to emphasize the main point or make a request.

THE START

1a

The first thing your reader wants to know when he opens your letter is, "What is the letter about?" Nothing is more irritating for him than to wade through half the letter to find out why someone is writing. Consider the following:

REGENT MANUFACTURING, INC.
173 Creighton Avenue
Chicago, Illinois

June 13

Mr. Terance Anderson
Anderson Placement Service, Inc.
148 Market Street
Chicago, Illinois

Dear Mr. Anderson:

A recent company-wide evaluation of our employees has led us to take a new look at our personnel policies. Thus, for the first time, we are searching for middle-management talent outside the company and would appreciate your referring to us any applicants you feel would meet our qualifications. We prefer college graduates but will also consider those with five or more years experience in administrating assembly-line production.

Suppose you have just received the above letter. Does the opening sentence give you a good idea of what the letter is about? *No*

. . . .

no

1b

Underline the sentence that does.

. . . .

X   *3.* A recent company-wide evaluation of our employees has led us to take a new look at our personnel policies.

  1. <u>Thus, for the first time, we are searching for middle-management talent outside the company and would appreciate your referring to us any applicants you feel would meet our qualifications.</u>

X   *2.* We prefer college graduates but will also consider those with five or more years experience in administrating assembly-line production.

1c

Using our answer above, rearrange the sentences by numbering them in the order in which they should appear.

. . . .

   2 A recent company-wide evaluation . . .

   1 Thus, for the first time, we . . .

   3 We prefer college graduates but . . .

      (These sentences, of course, would have to be reworded for continuity if they were to be used in an actual letter.)

2

Business letters are written for many purposes: to answer inquiries, to request information, to ask the reader to do something, to decline requests, to sell something, etc. Your opening sentence does not always have to make the purpose of your letter totally explicit, but it should always give a good idea of what you are writing about.

From which of the following sentences can the reader easily learn what the letter is about? _____

    A.   We received your letter of the 16th.

    B.   As you requested in your letter of the 16th, we are enclosing a copy of our

         booklet *Plan Ahead for Retirement.*

    C.   This booklet shows various ways in which you can ensure a comfortable

         retirement after only 15 years.

. . . .

    B

3

Sometimes, you may want to give away the whole purpose of your letter in the first sentence. For example, on the left below is a list of starting sentences which do this. Draw a line from each sentence to the purpose it reveals.

OPENING SENTENCES   PURPOSES

If you will fill in your name and address on the enclosed postcard, our representative will be glad to visit you at your convenience to explain our New Deal Life Insurance Plan and to give you a handsome cowhide address book—free of charge.

Because your 100 shares of Cetron Electric, Inc., have declined 30 points in the last week, we will need an additional $25,000 to increase your margin.

I understand that you are offering charter airline service and would like to know more about it.

Your order #5906V for 600 bushels of spring wheat has been put aboard the SS President Polk for delivery in early June.

to request action

to give information

to sell something

to request information

· ·

If you will fill in . . .   to request action

Because your 100 shares . . .   to give information

I understand that . . .   to sell something

Your order #5906V . . .   to request information

4

Below are five opening sentences. Which of them tells the reader what the letter is about? _B & E_

   A. I received your letter of January 19th.
   B. If you will fill out the enclosed questionnaire and return it to us, we will send you a free sample of our new cleanser, GLO-BRITE.
   C. At our sales meeting last week we discussed the possibility of a separate edition for younger readers.
   D. We are planning to institute a voluntary retirement plan for our professional staff.
   E. We no longer manufacture X62 and have therefore replaced your order for 20 gross of X62 with 20 gross of X63.

. . . .

   B and E

   (The reader's response to openings such as C and D is likely to be, "So what?")

5

Following are five sentences contained in a letter to a building contractor. Which should come first? _D_

   A. Due to expanded business, we need more space for our office staff and records.
   B. We would like to give the contract to a local company if possible.
   C. The building will contain 26 office suites for rental and five ground-floor shops.
   D. We are planning to construct a building on North Street and would like to receive your bid.
   E. Bids should be received before March 16th to give us time to reach a decision by May 1st.

. . . .

   D

6a

Your reader not only wants to know right away, "What is this letter about?" but he wants to know, "What's in it for me?" Thus, you should try to include in your starting sentence the idea that will be of most interest to the reader—whenever possible. Look at the following:

> I am happy to say that we have found a buyer for your house at an excellent
>
> price. He will be away on business for two weeks, but when he returns, he has
>
> promised to effect a closing immediately. That means you will be receiving a
>
> check for about $58,000 in about three weeks. Congratulations!

Does the starting sentence above tell the reader what the letter is about? _Yes_

. . . .

yes

6b

Does it include the idea of paramount interest to the reader? _Yes_

. . . .

no

6c

Underline this idea above.

. . . .

I am happy to say that we have found a buyer for your house at an excellent price. He will be away on business for two weeks, but when he returns, he has promised to effect a closing immediately. <u>That means you will be receiving a check for about $58,000 in about three weeks.</u> Congratulations!

6d

Rewrite the starting sentence of the above paragraph so that it not only tells the reader what the letter is about but includes the idea of most interest to him.

I am happy to say that we have found a buyer for your house, and ~you will be receiving~ *a check for about $58,000 in about 3 weeks.*

Congratulations! You will receive a check for about $58,000 in about three weeks because we have found a buyer for your house. (Congratulations!)

7a

Suppose you are writing a letter to an automobile dealer about a contemplated purchase of six new cars for your firm. Which of the following ideas should you include in your opening sentence? *C   F*

    A. a question about whether he has six cars in stock or will he have to order them from Detroit

    B. that he has a reputation for honesty

    C. that you need six new company cars

    D. that the cars will be used by your salesmen

    E. that he was referred to you by the district salesman

    F. that you are inviting a quotation of the best price he can offer

    G. whether air-conditioning is available

    H. that you are also writing to other dealers

C and F

7b

Which of these states the purpose of your letter? ~~E~~ F ~~B~~ Which is of most interest to the dealer? ___✓___

. . . .

F
C

7c

Write an opening sentence containing these two ideas.

I need six new company cars, and wish a quotation of the best price you can offer.

. . . .

I would like to invite you to give us a price on six new cars which we need for company use.

8a

Which of the following opening sentences not only tells the reader what the letter is about but includes the item of most interest to him? ___*A*___

   A.   Enclosed is our check for $1,500.

   B.   Thank you for your letter explaining the delay in the delivery of the X48 Road-Grader.

   C.   We are enclosing a sample copy of our weekly trade newsletter, "What's New in the Fur industry," which you can order for $6.50 on a six-month trial subscription basis.

. . . .

   C

8b

What is missing from Sentence A—an explanation of what the letter is about or a most interesting idea? _____*what the letter is about*_____

. . . .

   the explanation

8c

What is missing from Sentence B—an explanation of what the letter is about or a most interesting idea? _____*both*_____

. . . .

   a most interesting idea

   (Sentence A is a bad opening, but Sentence B may be perfectly acceptable since there may not *be* an idea that is of special interest to the reader.)

9

When you are replying to a letter, it is customary to refer to the date of that letter in your starting sentence. Doing so makes it easier for your reader to consult his original letter if he wants. However, such reference should always be subordinated to what you are writing about. That is, do not devote the whole sentence to the date reference.

Which of the following four versions of an opening sentence is best?

A. Thank you for your letter of May 16th.

B. I am enclosing the pamphlet you requested in your letter.

C. Enclosed is the pamphlet you requested in your letter dated May 16th.

D. We received your letter of May 16th expressing interest in our pamphlet.

· ·

C

(We realize that in some firms the custom is to refer to previous correspondence by writing the word ''Re:'' or ''Subject:'' and then the date or invoice number or whatever. This information is usually placed between the address and the salutation. If it is your firm's policy to do this, by all means follow that policy, but we will assume in this book that previous correspondence should be referred to in the body of the letter.)

10

I have received your order dated January 19th. Your six shirts will be mailed

within the week and should arrive before February 1st as you asked.

Rewrite the opening sentence.

The six shirts you ordered in

your letter of Jan. 19th shoud

arrive before 2/1.

· ·

Your order, dated January 19th, for six shirts will be mailed within the week
and should arrive before February 1st as you asked.

or

Thank you for your order of January 19th for six shirts, which will be mailed
within the week and should arrive before February 1st as you asked.

11a

Some letter writers have trouble getting started and consequently engage in a kind
of verbal warm-up, which is usually full of clichés, generalizations, or ideas which
are of no interest to the reader. For example:

<u>I am sorry about</u> the delay in answering your letter of March 2nd but I was on

vacation and have just returned. However, now that I'm back, your question

is easily answered; yes, <u>we do have a franchise available in southern Vermont</u>.

Underline the *two* ideas that should be included in the opening sentence of the
above paragraph.

· ·

I am sorry about the delay in answering your <u>letter of March 2nd</u> but I was on

vacation and have just returned. However, now that I'm back, your question is

easily answered; <u>yes, we do have a franchise available in southern Vermont</u>.

11b

Now write an opening sentence for this letter.

In response to your letter of March 2nd, we do have a franchise available in southern Vt.

. . . .

To (In) answer (to) your letter of March 2nd, yes, we do have a franchise available in southern Vermont.

12

Your opening sentences should contain:

1. an explanation of what your letter is about (including, sometimes, the purpose of the whole letter)
2. the idea of most interest to your reader, if possible
3. the date of his letter, if applicable

Each of the starting sentences below lacks one or more of the above items. In each case, write the number or numbers of the missing items next to the sentence.

___*1, 2*___ A. Thank you for your kind letter of October 22nd.

___*2*___ X B. Enclosed is a copy of the speech you requested in your letter.

___*1*___ X C. I have finally been able to talk to Mr. Palmer about your plans and consequently have some good news for you.

. . . .

___1 and 2___ A.

___3___ B.

___2___ C.

13

Which of the following are good starting sentences? _A & E_

- A. As you asked in your letter of May 6th, I am enclosing a copy of your article as it appeared in our September issue of "The Trackers Digest."

- B. Thank you for your recent letter.

- C. I have been going over the files for your account and am writing you about one of our invoices.

- D. In the process of merging Georgia Carbide & Atlanta Steel, many of the executive personnel were forced to resign.

- E. We have decided to advertise Gumshu on nationwide television and would like to know if you are interested in handling our account.

. . . .

A and E

(Sentence B does not tell the reader what the letter is about, nor does it refer to the date of the reader's letter; Sentence C is too vague; and Sentence D gives only the vaguest notion of what the letter is about.)

14

Suppose you are Director of Personnel and are answering a letter of inquiry, dated June 10, about openings in your company. The letter is from James L. Conrad, a recent college graduate who is interested in a managerial position. At the moment, the job of traffic coordinator is open. The usual hiring procedure is for the applicant to submit an application and then an interview will be arranged for him.

Write an opening sentence for this letter:

Dear Mr. Conrad:

In answering your letter of
June 10th, enclosed please find
an appl. to be completed.

. . . .

Your answer should include:

    1.   the item of most interest to him: the position of traffic coordinator is open

    2.   the date of his letter: June 10th

In answer to your letter of June 10th, we have a position as traffic coordinator open.

THE FINISH

15

One of the big problems for many letter writers is to think of something appropriate to say in closing. Thus, they often end with a vague cliché which is as time-worn as it is insincere. Perhaps the first person who wrote, "Please do not hesitate to call on us if we can be of further assistance," really meant it, but today's reader has seen it so often that he barely notices such words.

Which of the following endings sounds sincere? _____

    A.   May we again thank you for your cooperation in this matter.

    B.   Thank you for returning the forms to me so quickly.

    C.   Your prompt cooperation in expediting the above situation would be very much appreciated.

. . . .

    B

16a

One of the best ways to avoid the abstract cliché in closing a letter is to say something *specific.*

Dear Mr. Phelps:

Thank you for your order for 50 dozen LONGLITE batteries, which are being mailed via parcel post and should arrive no later than the 12th.

Which of the following is the best ending for this letter? _____C_____

    A.   Please do not hesitate to call us if we can be of further service.

    B.   Just give us a call if we can further assist you.

    C.   Just give me a call when you need more batteries.

. . . .

C

16b

Which of the above endings is the worst? _____A_____

. . . .

A

(Ending B above would be all right if Ending C were not better.)

17

Which of the following endings are acceptable? _____A-B_____

    A.   It has been a pleasure to be of assistance.

    B.   Let me know if there is anything more I can do to help you with your financial affairs.

    C.   May we have your check for $56.27 by June 16th?

    D.   If you have any further questions, do not hesitate to contact us.

    E.   Trusting we will hear from you soon, I remain, . . .

. . . .

B and C

18a

While the first sentence of a business letter is a good place for putting the idea that is of paramount interest to the *reader,* the final sentence is the best place for expressing an idea that is of prime interest to the *writer.* The final sentence is usually the easiest for the reader to remember. Thus, it offers an excellent opportunity for making a request for action, if that is the purpose of the letter.

Read the following just once:

Please accept my apology for our error on Invoice #16853. Enclosed is our Invoice #17864 for 30 gross of wooden spools to replace the one you received for 30,000 gross. Please return the yellow copy with your payment.

Because we just switched our billing over to a computer, we are still working out such bugs as the one which caused the extra zeros in your bill.

Again, we are sorry for this mistake and will make every effort to see that it does not occur again.

Without going back, what specific action has the writer asked the reader to perform?

_____

. . . .

to return the yellow copy with his payment

(If you were not able to answer this, we are not surprised, since the request for action is well camouflaged.)

18b

Now go back and circle the request the writer has made and draw an arrow from the circle to the place where it should appear.

. . . .

Please accept my apology for our error on Invoice #16853. Enclosed is our Invoice #17864 for 30 gross of wooden spools to replace the one you received for 30,000 gross. Please return the yellow copy with your payment.

Because we just switched our billing over to a computer, we are still working out such bugs as the one that caused the extra zeros in your bill.

Again, we are sorry for this mistake and will make every effort to see that it does not occur again.

19

I'm sorry but the *Diary of Alfred S. Potts,* which you asked for in your letter of April 6th, is no longer in print. However, we may be able to locate a used edition through our book-finding club which advertises in small magazines across the country. The charge for this service varies according to how many times we have to advertise but seldom amounts to more than $10.

Hoping to hear from you about this matter at your earliest convenience, I remain,

Yours Sincerely,

Rewrite this ending:

_____

_____

. . . .

If you do want the used edition, may we hear from you soon?

or

We will begin the search for your book as soon as we hear from you.

20

Below are sentences taken from a letter and put out of order. Which should come first? _____ Which should come last? _____

Mr. Thomas T. Evans
Director
Youth for Progress
Jennings, Texas

Dear Mr. Evans:

A. Although our company has not up to now made any effort to locate or train personnel from the hard-core unemployed, your report does suggest that we might find such a plan feasible.

B. Could you call me this week so that we can arrange to meet and discuss this further?

C. You mentioned also that you had information on the training staff and materials we would need to begin such a drive.

D. I read your letter of August 16th and your report with considerable interest since I had not realized how much was being done in a practical way to prepare the underprivileged to hold jobs in industry.

. . . .

D
B

21

Write a closing sentence for the following letter. You may extract information from the letter and use it in the closing sentence.

LEE'S DEPARTMENT STORE
Orange Tree Shopping Center
Reading, Massachusetts

April 3

Mrs. Dorothea Hicks
11 Maple Grove Street
Latham, Massachusetts

Dear Mrs. Hicks:

As you asked in your letter of November 5th, I am enclosing an application for a charge account. However, because it takes approximately two weeks to process, please return it to us no later than the middle of this month to allow you ample time to use your account for your Holiday shopping. We will call you when your application is approved and issue you a temporary shopping pass until your regular charge plate can be made up.

Please return this application at your earliest convenience for processing.

May we have your application, completed and signed, before November 15th (the middle of the month)?

22

When you are not requesting action from your reader but are simply supplying him with information, the ending of your letter is a good place to summarize your major points, especially if your letter is lengthy and detailed.

DR. JAMES E. PYNE
Director of Research
Chicago Institute of Applied Psychology
Rego Park
Chicago, Illinois

April 15

Dr. T. E. Holland
State Mental Hospital
Canton, Florida

Dear Dr. Holland:

About your query in your letter of March 6th concerning our current research in hypnosis, we are currently conducting a series of experiments on the possible uses of hypnosis in medicine. One experiment now under way involves 25 pairs of adults undergoing similar surgical operations at Chicago General Hospital. One patient in each pair receives an anesthetic before surgery and the other is hypnotized. We then compare them to determine if either method provides a faster convalescence and fewer postoperative complications.

A second experiment is being planned for mental patients currently in the care of the Illinois State Mental Hospitals. Again we will study matched pairs of adults, one to undergo psychoanalysis and the other hypnoanalysis, to compare the length of time required to return the patient to community life and the adequacy of his adjustment.

And we are considering a third experiment to determine the feasibility of using hypnosis to re-educate and re-orient the alcoholic, drug addict, and habitual criminal to a more productive way of life.

Which of the following is the best ending to this letter? ___*4*___

A. I hope I have answered your question and will be glad to keep you posted on developments as they arise.

B. To summarize, then, we are currently looking into the possible uses of hypnosis for patients undergoing surgery, psychoanalysis, and social re-adjustment.

C. If you have further questions, please do not hesitate to call on me.

. . . .

B

23

Write the closing for the following:

AXON, TELLER & WRIGHT
Attorneys at Law
333 Madison Avenue
New York, New York

September 7

Mr. John T. Warner
President
Reco Combustion, Inc.
721 5th Avenue
New York, New York

Dear Mr. Warner:

We met last week with Morris Filters' attorneys regarding your suit against them for breach of patent and tentatively agreed on an out-of-court settlement of $25,000. This seems reasonable to us, although, of course, if we prosecuted and won, we probably could get about twice that amount. The problem is that although you have a strong case, their attorneys tell us that they will request a jury trial, in which case the outcome is somewhat less certain than it would be if the case were heard before a judge.

Another consideration is the probable delay in bringing the suit to court. If Morris Filters wants, they can secure two or three postponements, after which, if we win the case, they can appeal to a higher court. Some of these patent cases have been known to take five or six years. If such were to happen, the consequent legal fees could leave you with less than the amount of the out-of-court settlement.

In conclusion, then, you can either accept the settlement of $25,000 or prosecute for about twice that at the risk of a jury trial and costly delays. We advise you to settle.

24

Complete the following letter:

JACKSON MAIL ORDERS, INC.
1148 14th Street N.W.
Washington, D.C.

May 6th

Mr. Howard Williams
Vice President
Rotary Printing Co., Inc.
Wilmington, Delaware

Dear Mr. Williams:

We are preparing a catalogue of our products and would like to receive your bid for printing, collating, and binding 250,000 copies. There will be approximately 108 5″×7″ pages, each with four illustrations; 48 pages in four-color half-tones and the remainder one-color; collated and saddle-stitched. As our mailing date is October 1st, we would like to decide by the end of this month to allow three months to complete the catalogue.

_____

_____

. . . .

May we have your bid by May 30th (before the end of the month)?

_____

25

THE GREEN BAY L.FE INSURANCE COMPANY
Automobile Insurance Division
15 Terry Avenue
Madison, Wisconsin

February 18

Mr. Peter Lowenthal
R. F. D. #1
West Redding, Wisconsin

Dear Mr. Lowenthal:

We have carefully considered your claim for $692.57 in repairs to your car which was damaged in your accident on February 3rd. Unfortunately, your policy lapsed on January 15th, at the end of the 30-day grace period which started immediately after the due date of your latest unpaid premium payment. During this grace period, we sent you two notices that your payment was over-due, but we did not hear from you. Consequently, your collision coverage lapsed and was not in effect when the accident occurred. Thus, I am sorry we will not be able to reimburse you for the cost of repairing your car.

Which of the following is the best ending for this letter? ___*D*___

A. If I can be of any further service to you, please let me know.
B. In short, you have been uninsured since January 15th.
C. If you wish to renew your policy, may I hear from you soon?
D. I am sorry this has happened, Mr. Lowenthal, especially since you have been a long-standing policy-holder with us, but I hope you will understand that we must stick to the precise wording of your policy agreement.

. . . .

D

(Sentence A is particularly inappropriate since the writer has been of no service at all. Sentence B is not necessary since the letter is fairly simple—it does not need a summary. Sentence C is asking the reader to be awfully reasonable, under the circumstances.)

This is the end of Lesson 4. Now turn to page 161 and take the Quiz for Lesson 4.

If your business letter is to be well organized, you must do some thinking and planning before you begin to write it. This does not mean that you should go through an elaborate procedure, especially if your letter is short and simple or you have a large volume of correspondence to handle every day. But it does mean that some preparation is necessary for almost every letter you write.

Thus, we recommend that you take the following three steps before you begin to actually write:

1. If you are replying to a letter, read it carefully and circle the important points you will cover in your own letter. Remember, your correspondent may not have expressed himself clearly, so you may have to read between the lines to get at what he is really saying.

2. Take some time to familiarize yourself with the circumstances surrounding your letter. In other words, obtain as much background material as necessary. Get the file of the person to whom you are writing and read any past correspondence that bears on the present situation. It may help to discuss the case with others in your office who may be more familiar with it. Find out everything you can about your correspondent. Is he an old, influential customer? Does he have a record as a troublemaker? And so on. The small amount of time you spend on research can save you much time and expense later on.

3. Jot down in a short list the ideas you plan to include in your letter. Then go over your list and make sure you have included everything you want to say and exclude those ideas which are irrelevant. Juggle the ideas around and begin to think of where they will go in the letter. Which ideas do you want to include in your starting sentence? Which ones at the end? How should the body of the letter be laid out?

   (This step may not be necessary or practical if you are already an experienced correspondent with a heavy work load. However, for those who are beginners or who have trouble organizing their letters, a "laundry list" of ideas may be helpful.)

Once you have taken these three preparatory steps, you are ready to actually write the letter. At this point, the main object is to get it down. Let the ideas flow freely and don't worry about your sentence structure or about whether you are being wordy or using too many passive sentences.

After you have got it all out, let it sit for a while and cool off. If you are dictating the letter, have a draft copy made up. Few writers can be really objective about a letter which they have just written. So, once you have let some time go by, then sit down and revise the letter so that it becomes clear, concise, natural, courteous, and personal. (It already should be well organized.)

If you follow this procedure for each letter that you write, you will find that the need for revision will eventually diminish as you increase your writing skills. However, if you feel that this procedure is not practical during busy office hours, take home some of the carbons of letters you have written during the day and increase your skill by revising them.

In the following lesson, we will give you practice in planning, writing, and revising some business letters.

REQUEST FOR AN ESTIMATE OF TIME AND COST

1a

Before we get into the process of planning and writing the letter, let's look at one that gives ample evidence that the writer engaged in little or no preparation before he began to write it. Read the following:

ARNOLD T. JACKLIN

Able Secretarial Service

14 Baker Street

Denver, Colorado

June 8

Jack's Typewriter Shop
57 Wytton Avenue
Denver, Colorado

Dear Sir:

(1) I recently purchased some used office furniture and equipment at a bankruptcy auction held last Thursday at a warehouse on Tremont Avenue. (2) In the lot, were some real bargains by way of office desks, chairs, etc. (3) Also in the lot I purchased was an old IBM electric typewriter. (4) As you probably know, these machines are pretty good if they are fixed up, and it appears that this one needs some work. (5) It looks like it has been stored in someone's attic for some time and probably needs a good cleaning. (6) What is your charge for this?

(7) By the way, one of my typists looked at it the other morning and told me that the ribbon does not wind properly and that the tab does not set. (8) In our line of work (secretarial service) we often do a lot of typing that requires the use of the tab. (9) How long do you think it would take to fix it?

(10) I am writing to several repair shops to get estimates for this job. (11) So I'd appreciate a prompt reply.

Look at Sentences 1 and 2. Do they give you a good idea of what the letter is about or what its purpose is? ___No___

no

(They relate some information in which the reader will have little or no interest.)

1b

Look at Sentences 3, 4, 5, and 6. These sentences do tell the reader something of what the letter is about and what its purpose is, but they are also filled with several irrelevant ideas. Underline those parts that are pertinent to the business at hand.

. . . .

(3) Also in the lot I purchased was an <u>old IBM electric typewriter.</u> (4) As you probably know, these machines are pretty good if they are fixed up, and it appears that this one <u>needs some work.</u> (5) It looks like it has been stored in someone's attic for some time and probably <u>needs a good cleaning.</u> (6) <u>What is your charge for this?</u>

(The ideas that are not underlined should be thrown out.)

1c

Underline the parts of Sentences 7, 8, and 9 that should be included in a revision of the above letter.

. . . .

(7) By the way, one of my typists looked at it the other morning and told me that <u>the ribbon does not wind properly and that the tab does not set.</u> (8) In our line of work (secretarial service), we often do a lot of typing that requires the use of the tab. (9) <u>How long do you think it will take to fix it?</u>

1d

In Sentences 10 and 11, the writer finally states the purpose of his letter and makes a rather vague request for action. In summary, this letter is disorganized and ineffective because the writer has included a great many irrelevant ideas and has not placed the relevant ones in the right positions. To revise this letter, first jot down the ideas that should be included. Do not write full sentences.

1. _IBM Typewriter_
2. _needs work_
3. _good cleaning_
4. _charge_
5. _ribbon doesn't wind_
6. _tab not work_

. . . .

Your list does not have to be exactly like ours, but you should have included pretty much the same ideas.

1. old IBM electric typewriter—just acquired
2. needs cleaning and repairing
3. ribbon does not wind
4. tab does not set
5. cost?
6. how long?

1e

Using our list above, write a revised version of the first disorganized letter. Juggle the various parts in your mind. Which ideas should go in the opening sentence? What should go in the finish? (If you prefer, dictate the letter and have a draft copy typed.)

Please provide us with a cost estimate on repair of an old IBM Typewriter. It seems to need a good cleaning, the ribbon doesn't wind, and the tab doesn't work. A response including approximate time and cost will be appreciated.

. . . .

Before you compare your revision with ours, go over it and make sure that it is clear, concise, natural, courteous, and personal.

Dear Sir:

I would like to have your estimate for cleaning and repairing an old IBM electric typewriter. The ribbon does not wind properly and the tab does not set.

May we have your estimate as soon as possible for the cost of the above work and for the time it will take you to complete the job? Thank you.

Sincerely,

Estimate of Time and Cost

2a

Now suppose you are Jack Pendleton, owner of Jack's Typewriter Shop, and you have received the above letter from Mr. Jacklin of Able Secretarial Service. Below is a list of facts and thoughts which you have jotted down in order to reply to his letter:

1. charge for cleaning typewriter is flat fee: $25

2. his letter: wants estimate for cost and time to repair and clean used IBM (date June 8)

3. replacement of rewind mechanism: $6 to $8

4. if tab set must be rebuilt, cost is $20–$30; if repaired, $5–$10

5. free pickup and delivery

6. about two weeks to do the job

7. we have three repairmen experienced on IBM's and one experienced on Underwoods

8. high and low charge for cost estimate: $36–$63

9. we have complete stock of replacement parts

Two items in the above list represent ideas which are irrelevant to the purpose of the letter. Which are they? _____

. . . .

     7 and 9

2b

Now begin to think of the ideas that will go into your starting sentence. Remember, you want it to tell your reader what your letter is about, to contain the idea(s) of most interest to him, and to refer to the date of his letter. Write the opening sentence.

_____

_____

_____

_____

In reply to your letter of June 8, I estimate the cost for cleaning and repairing your used IBM typewriter at $36 to $63, and we should be able to deliver it in about two weeks.

2c

Now write the rest of the letter, except for the closing sentence.

_____

_____

_____

_____

_____

_____

_____

_____

_____

_____

_____

_____

_____

_____

. . . .

We charge a flat fee of $25 for cleaning an electric typewriter. Replacement of the rewind mechanism will range from $6 to $8. If the tab set must be rebuilt, the cost is $20 to $30, but if it only needs repair, the cost is $5 to $10.

2d

Now write a finish for this letter which is as specific as you can make it.

_____

_____

_____

_____

. . . .

We have a free pickup and delivery service and will be glad to come and get your typewriter as soon as we hear from you.

_____

A CHANGE OF PLANS

3a

Suppose you are Manager of a new research project for a large pharmaceutical company. The goal of the project is to develop drugs to be used during and after open heart surgery. Your laboratory is in Annapolis, Maryland, but the home office of your firm is in Oakland, California. For the past few months, you have been trying to persuade Dr. Elvin S. Maynard, a brilliant but temperamental scientist, to move his family down from Cambridge, Massachusetts, to Annapolis and join your research team. In previous correspondence, you had arranged for him to bring his family down on July 10, 11, and 12 for an outing in the Annapolis area and for Dr. Maynard to inspect your facilities and meet other members of your team. You had planned to be at the airport yourself to meet his flight (510–American Airlines) at 11:30 a.m. on the 10th. Unfortunately, you have just been ordered to make a presentation of your project's aims and accomplishments to the Board of Directors in Oakland and will be away during the 10th and 11th, although you may be able to make it back on the morning of the 12th. Thus, there are two possibilities: Dr. Maynard can come down as arranged, and Dr. Howard Fastner, your Head Researcher, can take your place as host, or Dr. Maynard's trip can be postponed.

You are sitting down to write Dr. Maynard of the recent developments and to explain the alternatives. First, you jot down the ideas you want to include in your letter, as follows:

1. sorry, can't meet you at airport as planned on July 10th

2. your flight: 510–American Airlines due 11:30 a.m.

3. just been called to Oakland home office

4. make presentation of project's aims and accomplishments to Board of Directors

5. can't get out of it; it's a command performance

6. two alternatives

7. postpone your trip a few days

8. or Dr. Howard Fastner takes my place as your host

9. he is Head Researcher

10. will try to get back on the morning of the 12th

11. can do so by flying all night

12. can at least have a talk before you go back

13. let me know what you want to do

Cross off any ideas in this list which should not be included in the letter.

· ·

You should have crossed out ideas 2, 5, and 11.

(Idea 2 represents information that the reader already knows. Idea 5 is really not relevant because the very fact that the presentation is for the Board of Directors indicates the necessity of making it. Idea 11 is a little dramatic and might unduly influence Dr. Maynard's decision about what to do.)

3b

1. sorry, can't meet you at airport as planned on July 10th
2. ~~your flight: 510 American Airlines due 11:30 a.m.~~
3. just been called to Oakland home office
4. make presentation of project's aims and accomplishments to Board of Directors
5. ~~can't get out of it; it's a command performance~~
6. two alternatives
7. postpone your trip a few days
8. or Dr. Howard Fastner takes my place as your host
9. he is Head Researcher
10. will try to get back on the morning of the 12th
11. ~~can do so by flying all night~~
12. can at least have a talk before you go back
13. let me know what you want to do

Now begin to consider the above list of ideas in relation to the letter you will write. Which ones will go into your starting sentence? Your closing? Remember, you are very anxious to hire Dr. Maynard, so you want to present yourself and your firm in the best light.

Now write a draft of your letter and set it aside for five or ten minutes. Then edit it so that it is as clear, concise, natural, courteous, and personal as you can make it. (If you prefer, dicate the letter and have a draft copy typed.)

_____

_____

_____

_____

_____

_____

_____

Dear Dr. Maynard:

I'm very sorry but I will not be able to meet you at the airport on the morning of July 10th, as we had arranged. Unfortunately, I have just been called to our home office in Oakland, California, on the 10th to make a presentation of the project's aims and accomplishments to the Board of Directors.

It seems to me that there are two alternatives: you can postpone your trip down here for a few days, or, if you would prefer, you can come down with your family as planned. Dr. Howard Fastner, my Head Researcher, would be happy to take my place as your host for the 10th and 11th, and I will try to get back on the morning of the 12th so that we can have a chat before you return to Cambridge.

Please let me know what you prefer to do, and I will make the appropriate arrangements.

Sincerely,

SALVAGING GOOD WILL

4a

One of the most difficult tasks that you must face as a business letter writer is that of turning down a reader and still keeping his good will for your firm. No one likes to be refused, but sometimes you can salvage the reader's good will if your letter is as positive, reasonable, and sympathetic as you can make it. Here are several devices and techniques for making it so:

1. The first thing the reader wants to know from a refusal letter is "why?" Thus, it is extremely important that you give specific *reasons* for the refusal—when you can. Sometimes, of course, it may be necessary to keep the reason for the refusal secret, but most of the time you will be able to explain your decision in detail. This explanation should come *before* the actual refusal—to soften the blow. Above all, do not appeal to "company policy" as the sole reason for the turn-down. This usually infuriates a reader because his natural reaction is, "Why is company policy the way it is? You're just evading the issue." Remember, most people will respond positively to an appeal to their most reasonable selves.

2. Assure your reader that you have carefully considered his request (or complaint) by saying so and by making your letter *specific* enough so that it applies to the reader's situation and his only. Doing this will demonstrate that you and your firm care enough to take a little longer.

3. When you can, offer the reader *positive alternatives.* Often the situation is not totally hopeless and there are suggestions you can make to help the reader over his disappointment.

(cont.)

Below is a letter which says *no* to the reader. It contains examples of some of the techniques and devices described above. Read the letter and write the number of the device or technique next to the part that exemplifies it.

ALEXANDER UNIVERSITY

Freemont

Texas

May 11

Mr. James F. Monroe
10 Rivington Road
Pembroke, Virginia

Dear Mr. Monroe:

Our Entrance Board has carefully considered your application to our Liberal Arts School.

Mr. Toby, who interviewed you in February, was much impressed with your maturity and composure and gave you his enthusiastic endorsement before the Board. However, the Board noted that your high-school grades in English and French were below the standards we require, as were your scores on the language skills parts of the Scholastic Achievement Test. We have found over the years that in order for you to have an even chance to succeed in any of the Liberal Arts programs, you would need a higher degree of language and writing skills than you now possess. Thus, I am sorry that we cannot accept you next Fall in the Liberal Arts College.

However, I notice that you have a superior record in math and science. Perhaps, if you resubmitted your application to our Mechanical Engineering School, the Board would look more favorably on it. Or, if you are determined to take a liberal arts program, there is still plenty of time to apply at such places as Albany College in Rumston, Virginia, or Arlington College in Feldspar, Maryland, where the language skills requirements are more suited to your abilities.

Good luck.

Sincerely,

2

1

3

4b

Note the part of the letter which gives the reasons for the refusal. Does the actual refusal come before or after the reasons? _____

. . . .

after

(The blow of the actual turn-down is somewhat softened if the reasons for it precede it.)

REFUSAL OF AN ORDER

5a

Suppose you are the Manager of the Publications Division of The American Stock-brokers Association, a nonprofit trade organization for brokerage firms with about 800 members across the country. You have received an order for 50 copies of one of your publications, a book called *Analyzing Financial Statements,* from Mr. J. C. Toomey, Vice-President in the Credit Department, Peat-Warmouth Manufacturing Co., Inc., Pittsburgh, Pennsylvania, who wrote, "I have read this book, and I want every employee in my department to have a copy in his desk."

Because your organization is a nonprofit trade association, it is regulated by Federal law, which says that you can sell your publications only to your members—the 800 or so brokerage firms. Thus you must return Mr. Toomey's order unfilled. Nevertheless, you look at the list of your members and discover that there are two in Pittsburgh: Johnson, Phipps & Keys, Inc., and L. F. Rothschild & Co., Inc. It is possible for Mr. Toomey to ask them to order the books for him.

(*cont.*)

First you jot down the ideas you want to include in your letter:

1. have carefully considered your letter

2. thanks for the order

3. am returning your order

4. 50 copies of *Analyzing Financial Statements*

5. we are nonprofit trade association—with 800 members

6. Federal law says we can sell only to members

7. two member brokerage houses in Pittsburgh: Johnson, Phipps & Keys, Inc., and L. F. Rothschild & Co., Inc.

8. have them order

9. be glad to fill it

Cross out any of the ideas above that should not be included in your letter.

. . . .

You should have crossed out idea 1, since there is very little to consider. Federal law has made your decision for you. All you are doing is following it. Thus, it would be slightly untruthful to say, "I have carefully considered your letter." Also, you would not be entirely incorrect if you crossed out idea 4, since the reader may already know what his order consisted of. However, we think it should stay so that it may be used to identify the reader's order for him beyond a doubt.

5b

Now write your letter of refusal to Mr. Toomey. (If you prefer, dictate the letter and have a draft copy typed.)

_____

_____

_____

_____

(cont.)

_____

_____

_____

_____

_____

_____

_____

_____

_____

_____

_____

_____

_____

_____

_____

. . . .

_____

Before you compare your letter with ours, edit it to make it clear, concise, natural, courteous, and personal.

Dear Mr. Toomey:

Thank you for your order for 50 copies of *Analyzing Financial Statements.* As a nonprofit trade association for brokerage firms with about 800 members across the country, we are regulated by Federal law, which stipulates that we sell our publications to our members only. Therefore, I am sorry that I must return your order unfilled.

However, I notice that there are two of our member firms in Pittsburgh: Johnson, Phipps & Keys, Inc., and L. F. Rothschild & Co., Inc. I'm sure that either of them would be happy to order the books for you.

Sincerely,

ONE LAST WORD

Now that you have worked through the five lessons of this book, we hope that you will begin to apply some of the writing principles and skills that you have learned. For it is only through a constant effort of will and by continual practice that the writing of better business letters will become second nature to you. We cannot hope to make you an expert in the short time you have been working in the book, but you should have taken a large step toward becoming one.

Even more important, we hope that you have developed the right outlook toward the job of writing letters. Business letter writing does not necessarily have to be a burdensome chore. Rather we hope you will see the business letter as an effective medium for carrying forward your own career and for conducting the business of your firm. With this in mind, here is a useful piece of advice from Sir Ernest Gowers, who wrote some time ago:

> Be sure that you know what your correspondent is asking before you begin to answer him. Study his letter carefully. If he is obscure, spare no trouble in trying to get at his meaning. If you conclude that he means something different from what he says (as he well may), address yourself to his meaning not to his words, and do not be clever at his expense.

> Get into his skin, and adapt the atmosphere of your letter to suit that of his. If he is troubled, be sympathetic. If he is rude, be specially courteous. If he is muddle-headed, be specially lucid. If he is pig-headed, be patient. If he is helpful, be appreciative. If he convicts you of a mistake, acknowledge it freely and even with gratitude. But never let a flavour of the patronising creep in.

Now turn to page 165 and take the Quiz for Lesson 5.

QUIZ FOR LESSON 1

In the letter below, cross out all unnecessary, wordy, or redundant words or phrases and write in appropriate revisions where required. There are *ten* changes in all.

THE ACME FINANCE COMPANY, INC.
118 Orange Grove Avenue
Wilton, Conn.

January 28

Mr. Howard Williams
Williams Collection Agency
16 Willard Street
Stamford, Conn.

Dear Mr. Williams:

~~Please be advised that~~ we do not ~~in the normal course of procedure~~ *normally* use independent collection agencies. However, ~~due to the fact that~~ *since* each ~~and every~~ one of your references has given you an excellent report, I am asking you to take one of our more difficult cases, ~~which is that of~~ *regarding* Mr. Browning. In the last six months, we have sent him five overdue notices ~~in connection with~~ *concerning* his automobile installment payments but have not heard from him.

~~As a consequence of this~~, *Therefore,* I am sending you his installment-loan contract and other pertinent data, hoping you will have better success in collecting it ~~at an early date~~ *soon*.

I ~~personally~~ think that if you can resolve this case to our satisfaction, you can expect some more business from us in ~~about~~ two or three weeks.

Sincerely,

Clarence H. James

If you are working through this book on your own, you may score your Quiz according to the correct answers on page 169.

If not, your instructor will have the answers to the Quiz.

QUIZ FOR LESSON 2, PART I

Complete each of the following five sentences with the most *specific* word or phrase by writing the letter of your choice in the space provided.

1. Please be sure to sign the application ___ *A* ___.

   A. in the lower left-hand corner
   B. in the appropriate place
   C. near the bottom

2. You may expect your order to arrive in Detroit ___ *C* ___.

   A. in about ten days
   B. soon
   C. on January 10th

3. Mr. Phelps has made ___ *C* ___ contribution to the field of electronics.

   A. a significant
   B. a revolutionary
   C. a worthwhile

4. As soon as we obtain the necessary information, Mr. Conroy will ___ *C* ___ you.

   A. communicate with
   B. get in touch with
   C. phone

5. Mr. Lawson does seem to have a legitimate claim against the factory since the sidewalk in front of the main gate was ___ *B* ___ last Monday morning.

   A. unsafe
   B. icy
   C. hazardous

Rewrite each of the following passive sentences so that it becomes *active*. If the verb is *general*, replace it with a more specific one. You may have to make up a plausible doer of the action in some cases.

6. Completion of the project will be accomplished by the contractor before next June.

   The contractor will complete the project before next June.

7. Production at the Yuma plant has not been seriously hampered by the union slowdown.

The Union slowdown has not hampered production seriously at the Yuma plant.

8. Five copies of the manuscript were received two weeks ago.

5 copies of the manuscript were received on June 2, 1947.

9. The following letter from an instrument manufacturer's service manager to a customer who has asked for service on his Model M-2 spectroscope contains some passive sentences. Revise the letter by changing *all* passive sentences to active ones.

CARTER INSTRUMENT CORPORATION

Dayton

Ohio

September 16

Mr. Paul Whitman
Quality Control Department
MORRIS CORPORATION
Evanston, Illinois

Dear Mr. Whitman:

I am sorry to hear that you have ~~been having~~ *had* difficulties with your M-2 spectro-scope. ~~The problem has been turned over by me to~~ Harry Masten, our service-man for your area; *has refered the problem to nt.* ~~and you will be phoned by him this week to schedule a service call.~~ *He will phone you this week to schedule a service call*

I realize that your M-2 spectroscope must be operating to specifications by next Monday in order to maintain your production schedule. Mr. Masten also understands this, and ~~the necessary repairs will be made by him when he~~ *he will make the necessary repairs* ~~arrives at your plant.~~ *when he*

please ~~Arrangements should be made by you~~ to have a purchase order number ready for Mr. Masten to prevent further delay in accomplishing these repairs.

Sincerely,

If you are working through this book on your own, you may score your Quiz according to the correct answers on page 171.

If not, your instructor will have the answers to the Quiz.

QUIZ FOR LESSON 2, PART II

Fill in the appropriate links in the following:

1. The new production-line machines are more efficient _____*and*_____ more economical than the old machines.

2. We hope to have our hotel open for business by July 4th, _____*but*_____ we will not know for certain until at least the middle of May.

3. I advise you to put extra cash in tax-exempt bonds _____~~and~~ *or*_____ in a savings account, but not both.

4. Allied Mills, Inc. has been a valuable and reliable customer over the years. Lately, _____*however*_____, they have become increasingly slow in paying their bills.

5. All our life insurance policies have a grace period of thirty days in which a late premium may be paid without the policy's lapsing. Unfortunately, we did not receive your payment until fifteen days after the grace period expired. _____*Therefore*_____, your policy has lapsed and you will have to undergo a medical examination if you wish to renew coverage.

The following sentences contain faults in parallelism. Correct them.

6. All line supervisors in the Home Office will be given training in applying ~~and~~ *~~interpreting~~* the latest management techniques and ~~how to~~ interpret*ing* production data.

7. The girls we hired from the Office Temporaries Corporation are courteous, efficient, and ~~work hard.~~ *hard working.*

8. We have a plan in the works not only for expanding sales by 10% next year but also ~~to~~ increase*ing* profits by 20%.

9. Mr. Feenan interviewed the executives of Viceroy Company, Inc. on Tuesday, flew back to the office on Wednesday, and ~~his report was~~ *his report to me* handed in ~~to me~~ on Thursday.

10. I received your order for three Model X-54 earthmovers on July 22, and *I* ~~it was~~ immediately sent ~~by me~~ *it* to our sales representative in your territory.

If you are working through this book on your own, you may score your Quiz according to the correct answers on page 173.

If not, your instructor will have the answers to the Quiz.

QUIZ FOR LESSON 3

The following sentences contain examples of inflated language, archaic usage, negative words, and an impersonal tone. Cross them out and write in your revisions over them.

1. ~~It is deemed advisable~~ *I suggest* that you file your Declaration of Estimated Tax ~~prior to~~ *before* January 21.

2. ~~As was requested by you~~ *As you requested* in your letter of June 11, please find ~~herewith~~ enclosed a summary of the net worth accounts.

3. ~~As per our agreement,~~ *As we agreed* I am enclosing a check for $2,000.

4. ~~It is impossible for us~~ *We will not be able* to install your computer before next month sometime.

5. ~~Immediately~~ subsequent to the Bankers Committee meeting last Friday, ~~this writer~~ *I* talked privately with John Masters ~~with reference to a~~ *regarding a* promotion for you.

6. It is ~~always~~ a pleasure to hear that ~~someone like yourself has~~ *you have* been promoted to Vice President.

If you are working through this book on your own, you may score your Quiz according to the correct answers on page 174.

If not, your instructor will have the answers to the Quiz.

QUIZ FOR LESSON 4

1a. Rewrite the *opening sentence* for the following:

NEWTOWN NATIONAL BANK
Newtown, Ohio

January 10

Mr. Frank Ellison
R. F. D. #1
West Tyson, Ohio

Dear Mr. Ellison:

I received your letter of January 6th. In it you requested a refund of interest you paid on Note #6178. It seems our Note Teller calculated the interest using the higher interest rate instead of the lower one. I have looked into the matter and learned that you were perfectly right. He should have used the lower rate. Accordingly, I am enclosing a check for $56.28, representing the difference.

> I have read your letter of 1/6, and after looking into the matter, I have learned you are perctly wright.

1b. Now write the *closing sentence* for the above letter.

> Please accept my apology for this error in caculation.

2. Rewrite the *opening sentence* for the following:

    I would have answered your letter of October 25th sooner, but it has just arrived at my desk. In answer to your question about employment with us, we do expect an opening for an optical technician to occur in about six months.

    In answer to your letter of 10/25, we do expect an opening for an optical technician to occur in about six months.

3. Rewrite the *closing sentence* for the following:

    Thank you for your order of 30 West-Tec air-conditioners, Model #461. We have shipped them via Railway Express, and they should arrive in St. Louis by September 4th. If we can be of further service, please do not hesitate to call on us.

    Again, thank you for your order.

4. Rewrite the *closing sentence* for the following:

    I want to coordinate your efforts with ours so that we can complete the construction of the X11 prototype by August 19th. Specifically, I want to know if you will be able to complete the design of the fuselage by the agreed-upon target date of May 6th. I have to have your answer by February 20th, because our completion strategy depends on knowing as accurately as possible when your part of the project will be finished.

I do want to emphasize that we are more interested in quickly getting an accurate estimate of a completion date than in meeting the original target date of May 6th.

A prompt reply would therefore be much appreciated.

I hope to hear from you by 2/20.

If you are working through this book on your own, you may score your Quiz according to the correct answers on page 175.

If not, your instructor will have the answers to the Quiz.

QUIZ FOR LESSON 5

Suppose you are a Credit Analyst in the Credit Department of the Regent Pipe Company, Inc., a large manufacturer of steel, aluminum, and ceramic pipe and tubing. You have been reviewing financial statements and projections of the William F. Mauser Construction Company, Inc., which has applied to your firm for an increase in its credit line from $20,000 to $250,000 in a letter dated May 15th from Mr. Peter Carlisle, Vice President. The reason that Mauser wants the increase is that they have just won a million dollar contract from United Electric, a local utility company, to lay a 75-mile gas line. Thus, they estimate that they will need about $250,000 worth of 6″ steel pipe.

You have been familiar with Mauser for several years and are confident that they have the experience and ability to complete such a project successfully. However, in going over their recent financial statements, you notice that the firm is already heavily in debt. In fact, total debt is about $500,000, while the net worth of the firm is only $600,000. Thus, if Regent Pipe sold Mauser $250,000 worth of pipe on credit, Mauser's total indebtedness would soar to $750,000—$150,000 more than the net worth. This would mean that Mauser's creditors would have more money invested in the firm than its owners—a very unhealthy situation for a business in the construction industry, which needs to be financially in sound order to have the flexibility to meet unexpected contingencies. Thus, you must refuse to increase Mauser's credit line to $250,000.

In going over the contract between Mauser and the utility company, you note that it provides for a series of five progress payments of $200,000 each over the six months that the project is expected to last. You figure that if you allowed Mauser a credit line of $50,000 (i.e., they can purchase up to that amount of merchandise on credit), they could buy the pipe they need a little at a time. This way, total debt would not jump to such an unhealthy level right away. Instead, the income from the progress payments would allow Mauser to keep debt down as it went along.

Now jot down the ideas you want to include in your letter to Mr. Carlisle, indicating your decision. Remember, you want to keep Mauser as a customer.

_____   _____

_____   _____

_____   _____

_____   _____

_____   _____

_____   _____

_____

_____   _____

_____   _____

_____   _____

_____   _____

Go over your list of ideas. Cross out any that are irrelevant. Which ones will you use in your opening? Your closing? Now write a draft of your letter to Mr. Carlisle and edit it to make it clear, concise, well-organized, natural, courteous, and personal.

_____

_____

_____

_____

_____

_____

_____

_____

_____

_____

_____

_____

_____

_____

_____

_____

_____

_____

_____

_____

_____

_____

If you are working through this book on your own, you may score your Quiz according to the correct answers on page 176.

If not, your instructor will have the answers to the Quiz.

ANSWERS FOR QUIZ, LESSON 1

Below is the revised version of the letter in the Quiz for Lesson 1. The following
ten faults should have been corrected:

		Points
1.	Please be advised that	10
2.	in the normal course of procedure	10
3.	due to the fact that	10
4.	each and every	10
5.	which is	10
6.	in connection with	10
7.	As a consequence of this	10
8.	at an early date	10
9.	I personally think	10
10.	about two or three	10
	TOTAL:	100

Take off 10 points for each fault that was missed.

normally, usually
~~Please be advised that~~ we do not ~~in the normal course of procedure~~ use

because, since
independent collection agencies. However, ~~due to the fact that each and~~

every (or: each ~~and every~~) one of your references has given you an excellent

report, I am asking you to take one of our more difficult cases, ~~which is~~ that of

Mr. Browning. In the last six months, we have sent him five overdue notices

about, concerning
~~in connection with~~ his automobile installment payments but have not heard

from him.

Consequently, Therefore
~~As a consequence of this~~, I am sending you his installment-loan contract and

other pertinent data, hoping you will have better success in collecting it ~~at~~

soon, quickly, etc.
~~an early date.~~

(cont.)

I ~~personally~~ think that if you can resolve this case to our satisfaction, you can expect some more business from us in ~~about~~ two or three weeks (or: about two ~~or three~~ weeks).

ANSWERS FOR QUIZ, LESSON 2, PART I

Below are the correct answers for the Quiz for Lesson 2, Part I. Deduct the indicated number of points for each incorrect answer.

		Points
1.	A.	6
2.	C.	6
3.	B.	6
4.	C.	6
5.	B.	6

6. The *contractor will complete* the project before next June.   10

   To be correct, "contractor" should be the subject (5 points), and "to complete" should be the predicate (5 points).

7. The union *slowdown has* not seriously *hampered* production at the Yuma plant.   10

   To be correct, "slowdown" should be the subject (5 points), and "to hamper" should be the predicate (5 points).

8. *I* (We, Mr. Jones, This office, etc.) *received* five copies of the manuscript two weeks ago.   10

   To be correct, "I," "We," "Mr. Jones," or something similar should be the subject (5 points) and "to receive" should be the predicate (5 points).

9. Below is the revised version of the letter in the Quiz for Lesson 2, Part I. Four changes should have been made.

   I am sorry to hear that you have been having difficulties with your

   M-2 spectroscope. ~~The problem has been turned over by me~~ to   10
   (I have turned the problem over)

   Harry Masten, our serviceman for your area; and ~~you will be~~   10
   (he will phone you)

   ~~phoned by him~~ this week to schedule a service call.

	Subtotal:	80

		Points
	Subtotal:	80

I realize that your M-2 spectroscope must be operating to specifications by next Monday in order to maintain your production

                              he will make the necessary repairs
schedule. Mr. Masten also understands this, and ~~the necessary~~   10
~~repairs will be made by him~~ when he arrives at your plant.

Please arrange, You should arrange
~~Arrangements should be made by you~~ to have a purchase order   10
number ready for Mr. Masten to prevent further delay in accomplishing these repairs.

		———
	TOTAL:	100

ANSWERS FOR QUIZ, LESSON 2, PART II

Below are correct answers for the Quiz for Lesson 2, Part II. Deduct the indicated number of points for each incorrect answer.

		Points
1.	and	10
2.	but	10
3.	or	10
4.	however	10
5.	Therefore, Consequently	10

6.   All line supervisors in the Home Office will be given training in *applying* the latest management techniques and *interpreting* production data.   10

or

All line supervisors in the Home Office will be given training in *how to apply* the latest management techniques and *how to interpret* production data.

7.   The girls we hired from the Office Temporaries Corporation are *courteous, efficient,* and *hard working.*   10

8.   We have a plan in the works not only *for expanding* sales by 10% next year but also *for increasing* profits by 20%.   10

or

We have a plan in the works not only *to expand* sales by 10% next year but also *to increase* profits by 20%.

9.   Mr. Feenan interviewed the executives of Viceroy Company, Inc. on Tuesday, flew back to the office on Wednesday, and *handed* in his report on Thursday.   10

10.   I received your order for three Model X-54 earthmovers on July 22 and (I) *sent it* immediately to our sales representative in your territory.   10

TOTAL: 100

ANSWERS FOR QUIZ, LESSON 3

Below are the correct answers for the Quiz for Lesson 3. Deduct the indicated number of points for each incorrect answer.

		Points
	I think you should, We recommend that you, etc.	
1.	~~It is deemed advisable that you~~ file your Declaration of Esti-	10
	before mated Tax ~~prior to~~ January 21.	10
	As you asked	
2.	~~As was requested by you~~ in your letter of June 11, ~~please find~~	10
	enclosed is, I am enclosing, etc. \ ~~herewith~~ enclosed a summary of the net worth accounts.	10
	As agreed	
3.	~~As per our agreement,~~ I am enclosing a check for $2,000.	10
	We will, We will be glad to, etc.	
4.	~~It is impossible for us to~~ install your computer ~~before~~ next	10
	month sometime.	
	After, Right after	
5.	~~Immediately subsequent to~~ the Bankers Committee meeting	10
	I last Friday, ~~this writer~~ talked privately with John Masters ~~with~~	10
	about ~~reference to~~ a promotion for you.	10
	Congratulations on your promotion	
6.	~~It is always a pleasure to hear that someone like yourself has~~	10
	~~been promoted~~ to Vice President.	
	TOTAL:	100

ANSWERS FOR QUIZ, LESSON 4

Below are examples of correct answers for the Quiz for Lesson 4 and the instructions for scoring each answer.

1a. As you asked in your letter of January 6, I am enclosing our check for $56.28, representing a refund of interest you paid on note #6178.

or

The refund you requested in your letter of January 6th is in order and our check for $56.28 is enclosed.

or

You were perfectly right in asking for a refund of interest in your letter of January 6, and I am therefore enclosing a check for $56.28.

The opening sentence may be worded in many different ways, but it should include:

	Points
reference to date of the reader's letter (January 6)	10
mention of the check ($56.28)	10
subject of the reader's letter (request for refund)	10

1b. I'm sorry for our miscalculation; we'll try not to let it happen again.

The answer should include some sort of apology.	10

2. In answer to your letter of October 25, yes, we do expect an opening for an optical technician to occur in about six months.

The sentence should include:

reference to the date of the reader's letter (October 25)	10
idea of most interest (opening is available)	20

3. If you need more air conditioners, just let us know.

The sentence should include specific mention of air conditioners. It should *not* be a cliché such as "Do not hesitate to call on us should you need further service."	10

4. May we have your estimate of the completion date by February 20th?

The sentence should include:

mention of what is wanted (an estimate of completion date)	10
mention of the date when estimate is needed (February 20th)	10

	TOTAL:	100

ANSWERS FOR QUIZ, LESSON 5

Below is a letter representing an acceptable answer for the Quiz for Lesson 5.

REGENT PIPE COMPANY, INC.
Credit Department

Mr. Peter Carlisle
Vice President
William F. Mauser Construction Company, Inc.

Dear Mr. Carlisle:

Opening Sentence	I have carefully considered your letter of May 15 requesting an increase in your credit line from $20,000 to $250,000.
Reason for Refusal Refusal	In going over your financial statements, I notice that your firm is already heavily in debt. In fact, total debt is about $500,000, while net worth is only $600,000. Thus, if we sold you $250,000 of pipe on credit, your total indebtedness would soar to $750,-000—$150,000 more than net worth. I feel that this would endanger the financial soundness of your firm and hamper its flexibility to meet contingencies. For this reason, we must refuse to increase your credit line to $250,000.
Alternative	However, I am confident that your firm has the experience and ability to successfully complete the project for United Electric, and we do want to help as much as we possibly can. I notice your contract with United Electric provides for five progress payments of $200,000 each for six months. If we increased your credit line to $50,000, would it not be possible for you to buy the pipe you need in smaller quantities as you went along and use the income from the progress payments to keep total debt at a healthier level?
Conclusion	If this alternative is acceptable to you, please let me know soon, and I will make arrangements for us to promptly fill your orders for 6″ steel pipe as they come in.

Sincerely,

Deduct the indicated number of points for each incorrect answer:

	Points
Opening sentence should include:	
reference to date of reader's letter (May 15th)	5
subject of reader's letter (request for credit)	5
statement that request has been carefully considered	10
Reason for refusal should:	
be stated (indebtedness greater than net worth)	10
precede actual refusal	10
Refusal should be polite but firm	10
Alternative should:	
include offer to increase credit to $50,000	10
explain merits of the alternative plan	10
Conclusion should be specific, not a cliché	10
Deduct points as necessary for the following faults (to a limit of 20):	
unnecessary or wordy phrases	
over-general words	
over-use of passive sentences	
mistakes in parallelism or use of links	20
TOTAL:	100